Collection:wfp
Revised Edition

Collection:wfp
— Revised Edition —

A collection of words arranged by William Franklin Postle

Collection:wfp
— *Revised Edition* —

by William Franklin Postle

ISBN: 978-0-9849529-7-7
Library of Congress Control Number:
2015918492

Mundane Publications®
http://www.mundanepublications.com

FORWARD

COLLECTION:wfp is a *revised* compilation
of words I have arranged over the last few
years. There may be something here that
will move or amuse you. I sure as hell hope
so, I've put a lot of work into this. Find out.
My part's done, yours, if you so choose, is
just beginning.

Have you heard the one about the Arab
and the Jew? I have too, many times, and
I'm sick to death of it.

TABLE OF CONTENTS

The Classroom

The classroom is empty. The blackboard is wiped clean. The desks are clear, except for their carvings and deposits of chewing gum. If there is no one in this room, why is this observation being made? Answer: The omniscient author. Back to our tableau. The bell rings followed by ten minutes of silence. The bell rings again. Silence. No pupil ingress or egress, no teacher calling for order, no assignments scribbled on the board. The problem: I've selected a Sunday. A strange day to monitor the classroom. Why not Monday, Wednesday, or even Friday? Answer: I prefer the tempest of the vacant room, wherein swirls the whimsical dreams of youth, to the exclusion of exes and whys.

Take up

So, now that I've told you the story, what do you think? *What was it about again? Oh yea, The mom kills the pop and takes up with the oldest son. Don't you think that theme has been worked before, maybe a couple of thousand years ago by some Greeks?* Yes, true. But what I provide is the details, the sordid details. Exactly what was mom thinking the first time she was penetrated by her own flesh and blood? What was her son thinking when he ventured into the forbidden room from whence he came? Did he seek out the breast that once fed him? Were the lights on or off? Did their lips meet, did their tongues engage. Did she moan "I love you?" Did he? I tell it all: The sounds, the smells, the words, the guilt. I ask again, what do you think? *"Honestly, what I feel in uncomfortable. One is forced to put himself in that situation, and I just don't want to go there. Too conservative I guess. Have you any more conventional stories. Like say, the daughter murders the mom and takes up with the dad? This I can abide." You sir are a provocateur.*

I really mean it

I hate my brother, he's younger and sickly
and gets all the attention. How about me
family? I've got pimples, big stinky feet, and
sneakers that are last year's model. I am
forced to carry my lunch in a brown paper
bag that reeks of egg salad. This requires that
I eat my lunch on the way to school to avoid
being pilloried. It's always little Jimmy this and
little Jimmy that. I'm sick of it. I'm going to run
away, I swear, unless I get some respect. I'll
live on Hollywood Boulevard and let all kinds
of weird guys do all kinds of weird shit to me
for money. Hey mom, look at me now, get-
ting fuck in the ass for a living. Cry mom, cry.
Your first born has gone astray, and do you
know whose fault it is? It's Jimmy's fault, and
yours too. I hate you both. Take that God-
fearing family! And, as the Lord is my witness,
this time I really, really mean it!

Crying

I was murdered on the midnight train to Philadelphia. I know this because I was there. I remember it clearly. Lots of fear and regret compressed into the smallest corner of a millisecond. I didn't count on dying at twenty-three. Would anyone? I leered at her long and hard; see flashed a seductive grin. Her male companion took exception to these exchanges. Ergo, an eight inch blade inserted just below my diaphragm. My demise was exceptionally sad in that I never had the opportunity to touch those blushing lips. Had she squirmed beneath me just once, I would have gratefully accepted my fate. As it played out, I died with an erection — at least until my blood pressure dropped to zero. I know that because, as I said before, I was there. The train and I arrived in Philadelphia at the same time. We were both late. I was the last to disembark. After that, all that remained is total inky fluid darkness permeated by the provocative scent of a beautiful woman. Dry your tears fellow passengers, the train runs in both directions. Wake me when the crying stops.

Little Girl

She looked normal as a little baby.
Her body grew normally, her intellect did not.
Yes, I love her dearly in spite of her infirmities.
Had she been a normal child, I think I could
have loved her more. Is she happy? I sure
hope so. Could she be happier? Yes I'm sure
of it. Am I happy? Yes. but I could be happier
too. Maybe she will pass soon, a comfortable
painless passing. She would then be free to
be happier, freeing me to be happier too.
Yes, as I said, I love her dearly. But I'm sure I'd
love the memory of her far more dearly still.
And, I'd cry a lot less too.

From My Stoop

On my block, and the contiguous corners thereof, in my eighth year, was all the world I knew. From My Stoop, that world marched by, and what wasn't in the parade was close enough to hear, smell, or walk to. Each summer day, I would alternately sit and watch, or venture out to see how lives were made, how life might be, someday, for me.

The Milkman leads the parade. In the not-quite-light, the man-in-white, rattles bottles and grinds gears, bringing the day and dogs to life. Cryptic notes in glass bottles, chocolate milk with the cream unmixed. His sounds were the prelude to a Summer's day — a mid-summer morning's dream, music to a youthful ear, a glisten to his sleepy eye, a silent whistle to pursing lips.

The Breakfast of Champions, milk above the brim, the box-top in my pocket. I spooned with a measured haste, observed the obligatory chew rule, and did not gulp it down. All with disguised urgency, until I hit the back landing, sneakers half-laced, down the back steps three at a bound, in a race to my place out front — on my stoop, to plan my assault on another, too short, long Summer day.

Early on, The Junkman hitches his wagon to Phyllis, the old mare, and they creak and clop down the block in search of all things metallic. As they go, Phyllis leaves a distinctly non-metallic trail behind her. In that day, nary a thing was valueless, except maybe rotting garbage. All liquids came in reusable bottles, and those bottles had a deposit, newspaper, string, cooking-grease, the foil from inside cigarette packs, soup cans, rubber bands, bottle caps, popsicle sticks, steel, aluminum, copper, zinc; everything up to and including the kitchen sink. When the wagon rolled back in, after a long day of buying, trading and persuading, I'd slip over to see what was whole, what was not, and what parts were parts of what. And, to give some comfort to dear Phyllis. There seemed no joy at all in the confinement of that dilapidated stall. Why would there be? How could there be? Why shouldn't there be?

The Five and Ten Cent Store: Oh man alive, the things they had inside: amber tonics, Captain Marvel comics, penny bubble gum with picture-cards inside, balsa-wood gliders, kites wanting cloth tails, marbles, jacks, canning jars and wax, lead soldiers and articulating tanks for playing the game of War. I wondered at, and longed for, every single thing in that store. But little ruffs walking the aisles elicited no friendly smiles — not a place to tarry, just quickly wonder, and just as quickly wander out.

"Regs!, regs!" The Ragman shouts, pushing his wobbly cart down the block, bent over and dressed the part, his cries were part of the street sound fabric. What he did with those rags no one I knew knew, but the rumor had it, in a room beneath the Funeral Home just like Dr. Frankenstein's place.

I'd bet he wrapped dead bodies in the
Egyptian way, to preserve them for the day
when Pharaohs again held sway, and the
pyramids gave up their mummies to walk
the earth. Then, everybody'd wear sheets,
no underwear (They don't wear pants on
the other side of France!), have sand in their
shoes, and bow to some flat-chested old
dame with a long, neck and a funny name,
something like ... Never-ta-titty?

 Off to Uncle Louie's fish and poultry market
— the odor of fresh pike and warm blood,
fish scales flying like snow flurries, and guts
sloshing in a barrel. Grab a chicken by
the neck, slit its throat, toss it in a can, and
watch its blood and feathers fly in the
frenzied throws of death. (Once I thought
I heard a chicken cry, "How come God
won't let us fly?") Then, as if that weren't
pain enough, a funeral bath of boiling water
before the posthumous indignity of being
plucked clean, garroted, and hung out
for display. A great source of repugnant
fascination, this justified killing — this
suffering I could see, but not quite feel. Is it
possible they knew? The overpowering smell
of it all.

Behold The Sharpener passes, pushing his
most singular contraption: a unicycle with
a grinding stone for a wheel. Dangling
everywhere are fascinating tools for
sharpening everything that ever did, or ever
would, need sharpening. Oh boy, did the
sparks fly, like on the 4th of July, and in that
hail of fire, his hands never flinched, his face

never winced, so impervious to pain was this
man with hands of steel. When he finished
his honing, that edge was sharper than
sharp ever thought it could be. Hairs could
be split, and fingers too, and for just a nickel
or two. If you owed him you'd pay without
delay, "cause", they used to say, "he's part
Chippewa ya know!"

Next stop The Barber Shop: In a corner I'd
sit, well out of the way, listening to what
the regulars had to say, and how they said
it. Wondering … if I'd ever have stories like
theirs to tell, or be able to tell them in their
singular way, using cuss-words with impunity.
Sure, I knew them all, but what they meant
I, well … just can't recall. When forced
to, I'd get the 15/15 bob: 15 cent haircut,
15 second execution. The bowl he used
for a template was free, so were bigger
ears and itchy hairs all down my sweaty
back. He'd have his big belly all on ya,
and never stopped talking over your head,
without ever looking at your head. But,
so what! The indignity was short-lived, and
the onlookers enjoyed my gyrations and
the signature divots "The Big Clipper" was
famous for. Besides, where else could I get
so much grown-up conversation with so little
sanitation?

Make Lunch Time, the same time, every
time – right at noon, or … lunch would be
from the apricot tree. Four slices of white
bread, in between each pair, a lonely slice
of baloney, mayonnaise to help it go down,
a glass of milk and two cookies allowed in

the pocket for later. Ample chewing, always,
"Don't wash it down!", a ten second count,
then: "May I be excused, please?" Shoes,
stairs, back on the stoop to wonder, what
had gone by that had, in the interim, missed
my eye. When The Iceman comes by on hot
summer days, kids all trailed behind waiting
for him to throw back the canvas, unsheathe
his weapon and splinter a quarter-scored
100 lb chunk of ice into four melting glass
cubes. He'd bite a block with his tongs,
effortlessly toss it onto his broad, oil-cloth
covered shoulder, and head for an upstairs
icebox. While he climbed the stairs, boys
would descend on the shards like flies on a
dead cat. Relief from the heat didn't cost
a cent. Heck, there weren't that many that
even had a penny. Water and bare feet trail
the bearer of relief down the street, until the
next block's flock took over.

The Shoemaker's Shop's a favorite stop.
Sit as long as you like, with no obligation
to speak. The intoxicating odor of leather
and dye, wondering if the taciturn little
man, with deeply stained apron and hands,
ever swallowed those tacks stored in his
mouth like a chaw of tobacco. Hoping if
it did happen, I wouldn't be there when it
did. But, It'd sure be fun to hear what the
reticent cobbler would have to say. He beat
old shoes into submission, then granted
them new life, made heels respectable,
and saved soles. His work was never done
'cause, there was an endless supply of each.
All the finished work sat in the window —
shoes with new bottoms, and the same old

tops. No need to enter to see if your shoes were done, they'd be sitting in the window, up front, in the sun. When it was time for me to go, I'd just go, no words exchanged. I knew he liked, that I liked what he did, and I knew he was proud he did it.

The Corner Grocery Store: Campbell's Pork and Beans, Oatmeal and Cream of Wheat, Spam and pickled pigs-feet. Canned peas, and ... rats in the back as big as, or bigger than a cat. Present a list at the counter, soon, it all appeared before you. Of that gum and candy counter, you'd better stay clear, or you'll likely get tossed out on your dirt filled ear. They didn't trust little toughs like us much, and rightly so; for you'd never know when precious little Baby Ruth might be abducted, hidden out deep in a tyke's pocket for execution under some distant chestnut tree. We tried, really tried, to be good and stay clean on one day only — Sunday, and Jeez Louise, did Sundays hurt!

The Corner Tavern: Through its open door, breathed out stale beer and tobacco-smoke-air into the hot summer's mid-day glare. You could just make out who had lost their way and hadn't made it to work that day. There were the crocked walkers, the loud talkers, the over-friendly, and the under-friendly — looked like they were all having fun to me. Friday nights were family nights, and occasionally, our happy lot would shuffle through the sawdust for a fish-fry; to eat and gawk at the many colored bottles of mysterious liquids that made

people act in mysterious ways, and the tap's
golden flow, always stopped just so. All the
while longing for the day that I too would sit
at that bar, wantonly throw peanut shells on
the floor, order one of those little glasses of
caramel-colored stuff, take a deep breath,
throw it down without a swallow, until the
gulp of beer that would quickly follow, all
done in a single breath! Next, I'd light up
a Camel, take a long hard drag, blow the
match out with the exhaled smoke, slump
back with a deep knowing sigh, study my
dark in-need-of-a-shave Humphrey Bogart
countenance in the barroom mirror, and
softly proclaim: "Thank God ... it's Friday!"
With the nodding accord of everyone there,
I am reassured, all are reassured, that we're
in this thing together. What "this thing" is, I
would someday know. Right now, though, it
was too soon for me, those are things only a
man can know.

The Bakery Shop: Fresh baked bread and
cinnamon rolls, glorious éclairs, billowing
cream puffs, with beams of warm floured
light illuminating that sweetened sight.
The bread slicing machine, making fingers
tingle to watch it gnaw a soft compliant
loaf into that oft mentioned great invention
— sliced bread. The warmth, the friendly
conversations, powdered sugar on the lips,
bags opened before they hit the door,
weather reports and baking tips. Being
sent for a loaf of bread was a special treat.
(Although I pretended it wasn't.) On the way
home, I'd reach below the heal and remove
a still warm slice (or two), knead it into a soft

doughy ball, then pop it in my mouth. The longer I'd chew, the sweeter that morsel grew. A treat near impossible to beat. I'd shorten a loaf in that way, almost every day, and just between me and you, I don't think my Mom ever knew.

The Dairy about four doors down, was always good for a milk-can lid of cold freshly homogenized milk if I just did a little sweeping here, and mopping there. We called it a dairy, but nobody ever saw or smelled any cows there, just big shinny tanks. Where did all that milk come from? Always the silent observer, I swept, drank, and remained mute. But, I knew, somewhere, there had to be cows. With all that milk, there just had to be some cows, or maybe just one, a really big one, like Paul Bunyan's Lucy.

The Paperboy rides his route late in the afternoon, the envy of every kid in the neighborhood, on his Knee-Action Schwinn bike, earned from years of savings and new subscription contests. Please God, I promise to be good, just let me get my hands on one of those incredible machines. His route was long, few families could afford news in print; there was, after all, that most marvelous of all inventions — The Radio. When days were shorter and colder, supper was over and dishes done, off we'd all go for a radio show. But it's Summer now, there's no way Mr. Philco will have my ear while there's still some light in the almost-day-almost-night.

The Junkyard: From whence the junk-wagon rolled, was directly across from my stoop. Yes, believe it or not, just one hundred feet away, was the endless fascination of bins of oiled scented metal shavings, parts of everything, but little that was whole. Junk that was junk, but mostly junk that wasn't junk at all. The lonely old mare, back in her stall, after a long laborious haul, bowed and submissive, her eyes as yoked as she; grateful, as far as I could tell, for my comfort, and pocket's treat. There was so much there: the intrigue of the lost, sold, forgotten, and discarded — all right there to see, just thirty running, hopping, skipping, leaping, strides away from me. How darn lucky could a kid be!

The Cigar Maker: lived half way up the block. Occasionaly, I was permitted in through the creaking, fly-friendly, screen-door to observe how the most manly of all appurtenances came to be. From the stacks of aged tobacco leaves piled on the dining room table, dark stained fingers rolled, with spit and dexterity, elephant ears into stogies. Placing an elegant paper ring around each, he then laid them straight in a box, not just any box, the most coveted , and utilized, of all boxes — the Cigar Box! A work of art at least as splendid as the icons it contained. In the end though, it was the smoking that mattered most. The process: unwrapping, biting off the end, spitting it out carelessly over ones shoulder, rolling it the mouth, then applying a more substantial flame than any delicate cigarette could ever handle. The first thick plumes of engulfing smoke, the look of satisfaction, the robust manly odor, the ritual. I could barely wait to participate. Mr. Cigar Man never gave out samples, though occasionally, one would show up, to the dizzying delight of a select few adolescent puffers, rehearsing this most manly rite at some smoky clandestine site.

When the sun got low and the air filled with the commingled smell of food from many lands, I knew, my stomach too, is was time to go home for supper. Shoes parked, a reserved seat as the entire family meets, always plenty to eat, if you were on time. Seen but not heard, except for the occasional word, and that occasional word was always the same: with the first bite, "What's for dessert?", and after the last bite, "May I be excused pleeease?" Again shod in the hall, fly down that flight into the day's best part: the almost-night, the enchanted hour, day and play falling into gray. Kick the can, hide-and-seek, frantic play as if there'd be no other day. Desperately holding back the night with all your might. Please, please darkness, avast!

Then, the end. The mothers' voices blaring the signal for retreat: Bill-y! Edd-y! Johnn-y! Time to come in! It's time to come in! Dark is fun but I've got to run, or there'd be no tomorrow. Wash hands and face, put up with the howl about dirt on the towel. Saturday's a bath day: one tub of water, four bathers, and as the oldest, I went, not first as should have been my privilege, but last! (Could I have always been the dirtiest?) Lukewarm, gray water with a layer of scum on top. In my opinion, which I freely shared, I was cleaner before I went in, than when I came out. Did no good at all to stall. When the plug was pulled, and the water'd gone, well ... you coulda, with little care, grown Idaho potatoes in there.

What's the meaning of it all? The answer's out there, somewhere down the block, around the loop — from and back to my stoop. Everywhere stained, callused hands are busy shaping, reshaping, and mending the desperate parts of living into a usable, functioning whole. I studied it all in wonderment. Each night, I prayed the Lord my soul to keep, then drifted off to sleep, wondering over and over, and wondering again, what it would be like to be a man.

•••

The young boy pictured opposite was very often a welcome guest on "My Stoop". Although Robert (Bobby) may have asked himself the question "What's it like to be a man?", he never got an answer. While vacationing in Canada late that Summer, Bobby was hit by car and killed instantly. (So they said.). At his funeral, all I now remember is his utter waxen stillness, the spot of blood still remaining on his eyelid, and the almost unbearable weight of his coffin.

Yet —

I was a man
I did not cry
I did not say
Goodbye.

Flesh to Flesh

Dear Lord, save me from myself, simplistic
views, road-rage, idleness, fast foods. But
mostly, Lord, save me from religion, and
those who speak it: priest, preachers, dea-
cons, pastors, rabbis, bishops, ayatollahs,
popes — all hiding in the darkest corners
of the apse, where they perform their rites
and vale their souls. Lord, spare me from all
who would intercede on your behalf. Damn
them all! Destroy their monuments. Let's start
anew, just we two, just me, just you, with
nothing between mine and the divine. Ass-
hole to bellybutton Lord, asshole to bellybut-
ton. This way we really get to know each
other without contraception.

Ever After

I try for the pithy and satirical to populate pages for the sake of cleverness and form. What my heart wants there is different: romantic, mystical, shrouded things, beauty without bugs or thugs, Virgin Princesses and Shangri-La, Shelley. Schubert, and Monet, no bad breath or unwashed feet. Love complete, fulfilled and everlasting. Sorrow without grief, no rats or bats or body lice, innocent sensuous females, sans defecation, starched white shirts, manicured nails, tux with tails and forks for snails. Breaths of mint candy, delicate uncalloused hands, cathedrals where no word is heard. Glory in every story, told with infinite civility. Marriages and funerals with the same hopeful tears, a predominance of laughter, and happiness, now and ever after. What then will be written of it? Convoluted circumlocutions, peppered with arcane allusions, trailing reality into obscurity. Twisted grins and obscene sins at the behest of particle physics. And ... there are some who will call it Poetry.

Godiva Chocolature

A beautiful white lady rides an equally beautiful white stallion, her mouth crammed with chocolates. Dark carameled lips drip nectar down her chin, onto her rosy nipples, splatter her inner thighs, coming to rest commingled with her long silky tresses, and the steed's coarse mane. The lovely lady's low on chews, and is off, post haste, to the Chocolature. So urgent is her need, she hadn't time to dress and by this hasty mounting, woman, beast and chocolate commingle to stir her senses in a most rewarding way. Because of these rewards, below the hips and upon her lips, our pale Lady's trips increase in frequency, with ever increasing pleasure and ever increasing the measure of her girth to the dismay of her over-ridden steed. "If she does not reign in this habit", thought he, "she may become unbearable."

30

I Watched My Aunt Bea Die

I watched my Aunt Bea die. I knew she was
very close, ready, wanted to die. So I felt no
guilt in thinking, not of her as the moment
neared, but of death itself. So I waited there,
just she and I, for his arrival. I leaned close as
her breath became halting in anticipation
— he was at the door. A knock! (I could not
hear). She called, "Please, please come in."
(I could not hear.) There was a breath, then
two, a pause, then one, a pause, then none.
He had come, wearing a Hawaiian shirt
and an engaging smile (I could not see),
And giddily she went. As my eye blinked
she turned to cold gray stone. I wanted to,
but could not kiss the gray-granite surface.
Eagerly, I would skip a cold flat rock upon a
pond, but this rock would not skip, this stone I
could not touch. I found a nurse and said to
her, "My Aunt Bea ... she's turned hard and
gray."

The Door

I am a locked door, only that, nothing more.
What's behind me is, in truth, beyond me.
Why here, you ask, at the very back? I am, in
fact, a back-door, there is no other place for
me. Why locked you ask, if not a metaphor,
or maybe more? As before, I am a locked
door, and nothing more. I'm getting weary
and before any further query, there is not,
and never has been, a key.

Leave It

Wind and tree play together in a random
way. Sky is blue, temperature moderate, all's
right. Fair scene, a care-less scene, but, can
I leave it without comparing it? Wind and
the tree suggest to me: "What we do is not
for you, not a door or a metaphor. Let it be
what you see, and nothing more." Advise I'd
willingly heed, If I hadn't the need to find out
what this pair is up to.

Life is Sweet

The countrified have fields, and the meadow. The citified have pavement, and the parking lot. The meadow pulsates with color, the yearly cycle of life providing a bed on which to lie and watch the sky. The parking lot is white-lined blackness, radiating heat and a quickened beat when a parking space become available. Life is sweet along the street that borders the asphalt meadow. Elastic plastic stretches wants to needs, and no one pays till later, then refinances. But, the bucolic frolic is not all joy. They've added two lanes to the highway, there are more and more alien particles in the sky, more tears in the eye, and Wal-Mart just bought ten acres nearby.

Mall Bawl

Sometimes I want to lie down and cry. Not
cry alone, but in a crowded place. People'd
gather round and stare. "Look at that old
guy on the floor crying." "Hope it's not some-
thing too serious." "What in the world could
be wrong?" "That's so, so sad." "Best to
leave a sobbing man lie." So, someone'd
call security and they'd put yellow cones
up around me so nobody would slip on my
tears, and hurt themselves. The crowd would
then lose interest and disperse. So, there
I'd lie, alone with my tears, and the yellow
cones diverting traffic around me — no bet-
ter off than before I hit the floor.
Given this probable outcome, I think I'll do
my crying in my pillow, in my bed, like any
other self-respecting grown man would do,
and spare the Mall Crowd the inconve-
nience of a circuitous route to The Gap.

Lights

An empty office building, 4am Sunday morn-
ing with 27 floors and no people yet, there's
activity everywhere. Electronic phonics,
panels of lights burning brightly green, red,
yellow, white blinking, pulsating conversa-
tions among computers, clocks, telephones,
security systems, main frames. While we
slumber a binary conspiracy is underway
to hasten the day when scheming bits and
bytes will abscond with our rights and re-
place them with 1's and 0's. Then, we'll be
confined to the charged cages of electronic
sages who circle the sky tirelessly, wirelessly
ruling the world with Binary-Tequila in the
bars, and customer support from Mars.

Parts

Substance follows form legato, staccato,
lyric ingress, percussive egress. Delight
the mind with pastel landscapes. Find the
hidden bower door, open that secret portal
and reveal neatly stacked baby-body-parts
on a manicured lawn. Ah yes, waken him
from his afternoon nap, with a slap in the
face, use an oaken paddle covered with
fly-paper, covered with flies. With dislodged
jaw, and fly-ed brow, the accosted wonders,
"What was I dreaming about?" If this is his
query, then you, my friend, have failed to
awaken him.

The Making of a Hero

First date: wrestling tongues, drinking,
smooching, groping, drinking, writhing in her
room, seeking all orifices in a daze, drinking,
fumbling, passing out. The next morning, I
wake to her tears —she is moved. I didn't try
penetration, so respectful was I of her, she
thinks. A booze disabled cock and brain,
and now I'm a hero. Should I fuck her now,
right through those grateful tears? Why
should a hero have to wait to get his medal
on a second date? Hell, there might not
even be one. So parting that veil of tears
I plunged into the midmorning darkness.
She moaned, shuttered and finally smiled.
She came, I came, she came, I came, the
making of a Superhero, and all before noon
(just), hung over too, and before I'd even
brushed my teeth. By one o'clock , I'm gone
from under the weight of tear-dampened
sheets, and into the throbbing midday sun.
I'm sorry, but that's the end of that, I just
can't respect a girl who lets you fuck her on
the morning after the first date.

Measuring

What matters most to you? Time. *Of all things, it's time that matters most to me.* You certainly don't mean that time is more important to you than your own family? *Yes. If what matters most is that which most occupies your mind, then it is Time.* You do understand that Time is the one thing over which you have absolutely no control? *Yes, and still I am obsessed with it, the nature of it, the relativity of it.* What single aspect of Time engages you the most? *Its illusiveness. To quote a here-to-fore unknown poet: "I stood still, I concentrated, I waited, and I missed it."* Well, I guess that's the great mystery: The evidence of Time's presence is everywhere, but Time itself is nowhere to be found. That's the fascination. *As I lay dying, I will focus on 'The Interval', and try to understand and quantify it. 'The Interval', being the sequence that begins with my last breath, and ends with my final sigh.*

Not Real Lives

He walks up to her, there is a short,
subdued verbal exchange, and they
part. That was the first time they met,
and the last time, till now. Why do
they deserve mentioning here? They
don't. They haven't earned their just
deserts. They are not real people.
There was no real encounter. But, with
each line I write, they become a little
more real-like. Who am I to create
a man and a woman and deprive
them of a past, present or future; no
failures, no problems, no families? Well
hell, the Heavenly Father does that
all time. He not only populates the
world with hes and shes with no past,
present or future, but he encourages
them to procreate. Better I create
these hes and shes. I will give these
not-real-people a life without real
suffering, real problems, or real failures,
although, their not-real-lives have
them in abundance. How sweet for
them to wade through hell and high-
water without pain or consequence.
He meets her, they speak, separate,
but meet again, and again, fall in
love, do the family thing, live and die,
as the middle class does with sufficient
drama to make a compelling story.
Their story was not a best seller, but
those who did read it saw something
of themselves in it, not knowing that
neither of the protagonists had a life
—a real life, of their own. But ... that
never seems to matter.

Orange

Everything grouped together in
uncommon associations — a still-life.
A bowl, the color of an avocado, if
an avocado was ever a single color.
Inside that bowl are two apples,
each the same different color: an
apple colored apple-green, and an
apple colored apple-red. There are
three bananas too, each a different
banana color: banana yellow with
black lines and spots in exactly the
right places, differently placed on
each. Thirdly, is a single orange. A
single unwed orange-child thrown
together with fruit he knows are not his
siblings. The orange is a proud orange,
as proud an orange as an orange
can possibly be. He is, in color, I can
say it no other way, the essence of
orange. And, this essence stole the
show, winning the blue-ribbon-blue,
blue ribbon. The avocado bowl came
in second (I know), the two apples
tertiary, and the bananas lastiary.
Can you see it, the still-life I have so
artfully described? The bananas,
apples, and orange, gathered in an
avocado bowl, so vivid, so real, so still
in their decomposition.

Purpose

Cut a piece of rope to a length of three feet. Tie a knot in the middle. Pull that knot as tightly as you can. Examine what you've done. Now, try to untie that knot. Keep trying until you succeed. It may take a while. Now examine what you've undone. Beyond creating a three foot length rope, Did anything really happen? Was anything really done, or undone? What evidence do you have of it? "I have this, what you have written here — your directions to me, which I followed to the letter. Is this the evidence you require, or am I missing something?" Yes, you are missing something.

Stones

Archeologists want to know the how and the when of the earliest men, as men die around them for the same how and when they seek. Pyramids and Temples on the backs of those and them — these men do give a damn about history's judgments. The elite are treated to books, and the ones that did are done before they begin, die and are forgotten, with no stone for what they did. They: the how and the when, carried the monuments on their backs laid the tracks, mined the glitter, drilled the black, stuffed the holds with glory and themselves, and never ever got a piece of pie, on a plate, or in the sky. Slave keepers and slaves, in a ratio of ten million to one. The one is history, the ten million are offal. The offal feeds the furnaces, heating the genius of our kind. The ten million wait beneath the dirt, are the dirt, in the dirtiest joke all — a posthumous mention somewhere, anywhere, in the accounting of man. They are waiting now, an ever swelling throng wanting to know how, wanting to know when.

Summing Up

It's Spring and War, and almost everything's
in bloom — well, not everything, just the
precocious ones. The Future looks bright, not
glaring, a diffuse glow. The weather's fine,
not a perfect day, or anything approaching
a perfect day, but acceptable for this time
of year. Basically, well ...everything is ...
nice. A lot closer to nice, than not nice. All
and all, it's a Spring I can live with, as if I
had a choice. So, what's next? It's Summer
and War that's next, with long days and
hot weather complaints, evening walks,
out of necessity, cooler outside than inside.
Burgers on the grill, cooked too much or
not enough. Corn-on-the-cob for those with
their own teeth, and corn-off-the-cob for
those who haven't. Traffic to the beach,
the beach, traffic back from the beach —
in that order and in equal amounts. Sand
from the beach, no longer at the beach.
Nice, a little on the hot side, but nice as
Summers go. So, what's next? Fall and War
is all, and school again and kids back off
the street, and back in the classroom where
they should be 24/7. Christmas advertising
starts, each year a little earlier, going directly
from beach balls to tree lights. Autumnal
colors, in some colder places, but not
where I live. Trick-or-treating, and hiding in
the back bedroom with all the lights out
till the menace has past. Busted pumpkins
and some rain, but not where I live. Fall's
no masked ball, but I can get through it.
So, what's next? Now, it's Winter and War
that follows, as is the usual progression,

with maxed out credit cards, idol worship and irresolute resolutions. Family giving and getting and whining and complaining. Lights up, lights down. A new Year dawning, with yawning in front of the HDTV. It's all so exciting sure, but, isn't there more? What's next? Just war is all. Then another Spring, Summer, Winter and Fall.

•••

The Dresser

The sun rose, I rose, I didn't see the sun rise,
but, I saw the me-rise, in the dresser mirror.
Better, I'd seen the sun rise. That god-
damned mirror. Wood and glass forever
sitting on its ass collecting dust and trust.
Ever the photojournalist, documenting
the demise of youth. Oh the pane of that
exposé. Could I avoid it all by sleeping in
the hall, or keeping the bedroom dark? He
wouldn't care, he's got relatives everywhere
doing the dirty work for him. I'm sure that in
time his interest will abate. And to hasten
the rate, I never miss a chance to deflect his
glance with one particular stance: Standing
bare, I face away from his stare, reach for
my toes, and reveal to his prying eye a sight,
even he is loath to reflect upon.

I need to add some fire power to my poetic
arsenal. And where, I ask myself, is that fire
power going to come from? The Inferno
of my mind, I respond. (There's that stupid
grin again.) It's (the inferno of my mind)
at the present time flickering. Low on fuel,
yellow impotent flame, undercooked meat,
parasites, sickness, loss of creative life,
sending me back onto the sofa to watch
reruns of reruns — a flat-on-my-back-attack
of the first order, accompanied by an eating
disorder of the first order, and a second
order and a third order. The source of this
infirmity? Unresolved Conflict. Which came
first, the chicken or the egg? It seems logical,
breakfast precedes all other meals, eggs
are a breakfast food, no one eats chicken
for breakfast, ergo the egg precedes the
chicken. You and I both know this is spurious.
What obstructs my creativity is gluttonies
physical manifestation. My reflection is a
curable affliction. The course of treatment
is this: Special mirrors will be installed
throughout my domicile that distort, like
those fun-house mirrors at the carnival. Now,
since my body is, itself, severely distorted,
the result of distortion reflecting distortion
should be, it seems to me, a perfect
symmetry. (Minus times a minus equals a
plus.)I proceed with this plan, but then,
guess what, during installation, my dead
parents show up, and start re-advising me
about how to live my life, with the very same
skewered advice they fucked me up with

when we went around the first time. Then, they wanted me to live right, they now, postmortem, want me to live what's left of my life, right. I have always, and will always, live my life well to the left of right. How about living life up, or down, or all around — how about those alternatives, dear dead Mom, dear dead Dad? Decomposing oldsters, please go back to whence you came and continue to disassemble. It's my turn to self-destruct, not the right way, the left of right way: With an overstuffed me, on an overstuffed settee, the refrigerator for a lamp table, the door handle oriented just so. (Twisting's a bitch, too much of which can get one in traction, severely limiting one's inaction.) Well, anyway, now that I've gotten rid of my dearly beloved in-parts-parents, there is just me, my sofa, refrigerator, lamp (for the non-illuminating remote), a 60 inch HDTV and a couple of stinking pillows. I'm set for life. Who shops, you might ask? My wife shops, I might answer. You have a wife? You might ask. Yes, I indeed have a wife, I might respond. She has her own room, set up just like mine, and we communicate by cell phone. We have a shopping service, and someone comes in three time a week to change the sheets and empty the bed pans. (They won't touch my pillows though.) So, my friend, there you have it, joie de vivre safely nestled in cellulite. I have come so far in this artless life. I used to run around aimlessly, like a fool, seeking answers to unanswerable questions, (Which came first, the chicken or the egg?), and obscuring the

answerable ones. I don't do that anymore. Ha-ha ... I can't do that anymore. I am in total control, doing what I want to do, and doing it my way. So Mom and Dad, and all critics of my lifestyle — kiss my fat, blue-white ass! You can't miss it. But first, [grunt] let me roll over on my side, so that I may observe, without distortion, the frogs kissing the Fair Prince's gluteus maximus. *What about spontaneous immolation?*
What about it. Can you eat it? Can you cook with it? Can you sleep on it? Can you channel-surf with it? As I rest, I rest my case. You laugh at me, I laugh t you. For me, it's not a painless thing to do.

***

The Tank

Yellow tank-top and blue shorts, trying
hard to cover what desperately needs
covering, if covering undulating roles
and random bulges is a priority to you.
Hair monochromatic and everywhere.
Open toe shoes revealing overlapping
tortured metacarpals. She's so, so...in
need of combat boots. A full regalia of
combat attire, including gasmask, might
be appropriate — Haute couture for the
misconfigured, sans lethal accessories. Her
appearance itself, might be considered,
by some (GWB) a "weapon of mass
destruction". Her carriage has a loose
wheel. She shimmies in defiance of the laws
of physics. Her other carriage, the carriage
she is pushing, has something in it. I dare
not look, for fear ... That's it, I dare not look
for fear! There are sounds coming from in
there. Sounds like the sounds of something
eating something that's still alive. I dare not
go near. Why am I attacking this formidable,
yet guiltless woman? Would she not kick my
ass all over the parking lot if she knew what
I'm writing? Truth is, I'm a narrow-minded
coward, but, a svelte, stylish coward, and
as such, I reserve the right to shamelessly
ridicule affronts to my sensibility. I try not to:
imagine her naked, jumping rope. I try not
to: imagine her in a string bikini. I try not to:
imagine her trying to wipe her ass. Does
prurience carry me there, to think of not
thinking those things? I sure as hell hope not!
Forgive me Lord, for I have sinned. (And, by
God, so has she.)

The Voice

I drive in the fast lane. No, I pretend to
travel the fast lane when in fact, I stroll a
country road; specking endlessly to my dog,
and the frogs, and any other non-human
that can understand and not respond. An
unrestrained solilocuy to purge my soul.
Yet there is this inner voice I cannot reach.
A voice that tells me who I am and what
is acceptable to think. When I rant aloud,
alone, those words are adjusted for form,
content, and acceptability by the source of
the inner voice. Acceptable to whom? The
dog or the frog? No, to me! I hear what I'm
about to blurt, before I blurt, and thereby
sensor the extemporaneous. There is no
cleansing. No words that cause a shudder
or revulsion, or revelation. There is an editor
there, somewhere, screening every whim
and impulse for impropriety. When I speak,
the voice I hear is not the voice I want to
hear. The voice I hear is that of a coward.
Will it always be this way? Will the lamb ever
be able to roar?

Admission 99cents please.
Sorry, I don't have change now,
catch you after the show.

99 Cents Worth

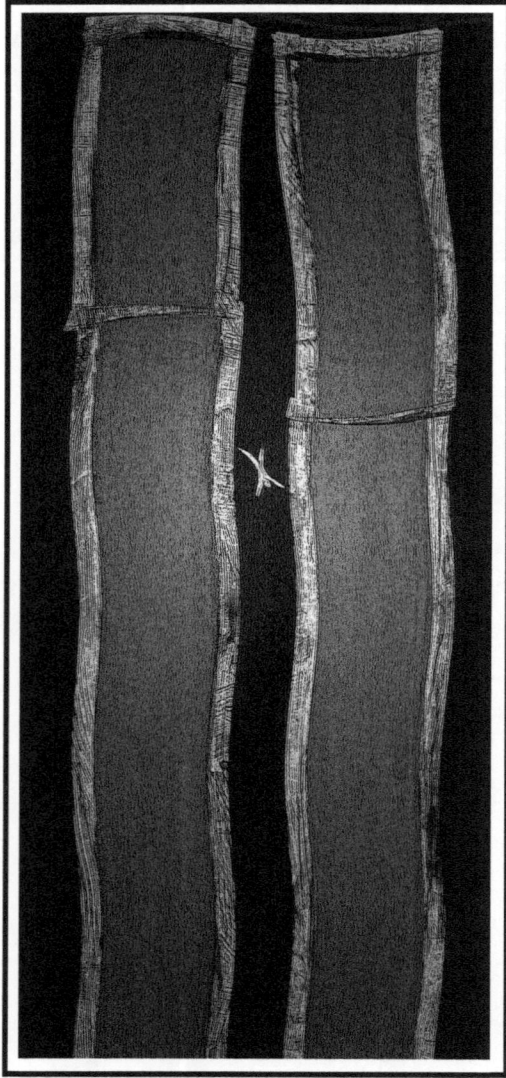

Emptiness: Empty churches and arenas, train stations and office buildings. Places where people gather but do not live. Times when there are no gatherings there. Times in between times. Structures like those times alone to echo and reflect. The empty house though, longs for occupants, never seeks solitude. An abandoned house is joyless, creaking, moaning, crying out to harbor and protect, what they were born to do. Sadist of all, the dwelling never occupied, waiting to die without memories, like an unworn wedding dress buried in a cedar chest. Or sadder still, that same dress hung in the closet of a house that never knew laughter or a Christmas tree. [The builder ran out of money and the development never fully developed.] Ecstatic over the prospect of a new home, the bride-to-be, between the engagement and the wedding day, ate her way from a size eight to a size eighteen. The groom in turn went from engagement to disengagement and was last seen heading out of town with the Maid of Honor face down on this lap. About a year afterward, we caught up with the jilted bride and asked her if there was a chance she might be wearing that wedding dress any time soon. "Fat chance!" was her wry replay.

Alone

There is this section of the world out back,
between warehouse and railroad track:
gravel, weeds, rusting beer cans, chunks of
styrofoam, dry, hot and separate. Flat cars
with shipping containers raise dust and bend
the wild mustard with a loud racket no one
hears. I visit that fallow place often, with its
meaningless remnants, it suits my memories
and ambitions. The train never stops here
and the ants cannot stop here. There the
wayward butterfly does not ask, does not
demand. There between concrete and rail,
where the debris of living congregates and
speculates on the future of an unspent pen-
ny lying fearfully on the vibrating track.

Beauty

Tall and straight, I cannot wait for her an-
gular form to articulate. Delicately rounded
edges draped in soft cotton, this exquisite
form moves like the slow measures of the Bo-
lero. She pauses to rest in motionless grace,
The music never ceases, the longing only
increases.

Blame

As sunny days go, this one's fine. No shattered bodies lying around except for LA's normal ration of traffic fatalities, homicides and suicides. No car bombs exploding, no brainless politician's rationalizing death and chaos at this moment in my ear. I'll take this bright day with its warm breezes and petty peeves, far from the inane violence we at once condemn and participate in. Then, red ink leaks from my pen, staining the pocket of my bright white shirt. Shit! Simultaneously, bright red arterial blood spurts from a young soldier's chest staining the hot sands of hubris. Now, bend over this boy, close enough to smell his failing breath. Now lie to him. Say to him in this final moment of his life, say this to him: "It's over, and we have won."

Chained

As a tear falls a year falls and many more of each will follow to call us up to lie down and accept our sorrow — what we wish to forget cannot be forgotten. After time has erased our name and countenance from all living memories, it will still live on as part of the wind, filling the sails that drives men's ships upon the reef of everlasting grief. Look up my shipwrecked fool. On redeeming sand you sprawl. Eden's here. Lost place, found man. Rise and walk out, away over the berm and into the shadowless valley. Build a hut of sticks and stones mortared with your regret. Do not cross the threshold yet. A monument to what's past, your building's done. Move out, through the past plunge, to the reef upon which you did last founder. Climb up the crags to the sentinels post. This is where your place will be, beaming caution out to sea, warning all ships of wayward fools to stand clear. You may, if you wish, return to shore. In that vale, the house you built waits, longing to echo your wailing remorse on yet another wayward course.

Girls in Flight

Lithe ladies of the day on their way projecting a ray that lightens the day as nothing else can. Bright eyes filled with enticement's smiles and the excitement of forthcoming passions. Dressed any way at all, it makes no difference what they wear, vales enhance the mystery. They glide about, chattering zephyrs on a warm summer day. They drift without effort. I long to fly with them, to share what is and what is not, what I remember, and what I cannot. They are elegant and new in everything they do, delightful in all ways, innocent of failure. They leap artfully out of adolescence — would they not. Stay right there, in midair, suspended between now and then.

Crossings

Intersections, where people come together but no one meets. Green, yellow, red. Go, caution, stop, wait. Then quickly on to the next encounter, where again no one ever meets, except in tragedy.

What Matters

Size matters, fat matters, toothlessness matters. Color matters, ethnicity matters, your car matters, your clothes matter. Every single element of your appearance matters. And anyone who tells you differently ... even if that person happens to be an overweight, toothless, albino Tutsi little person, dressed in tatters, and driving a 1980 Toyota pickup with bald tires, he, maybe more than most, matters too.

In L.A.

One gray day, tha⁻'s OK. Two gray days,
near intolerable. A third gray day has a way
of darkening the promise. A forth gray day,
no way can we survive so sad a sequence.

Gone

Today is … well, just another day, but is counts. Time is … just time but it mounts. It's June and the sun is high. Stop to reflect and Summer's gone by. What's going on? What was near is gone, what's just past is forgotten. Where is tomorrow? Intensely focused, I stand perfectly still determined to watch time's passing … I wait and wait … and I miss what's gone by.

Good Lard

A pound of lard way back in the cupboard.
What's this about. There amongst all the
non-fat, low-cal, no-cal, instant flavorless-
ness it hides itself from the modern day cook.
It once could be found 24/7 in a cast iron
skillet, on the back of the stove with a layer
of grease that would never decrease and
the tastes and smells of everything it ever
browned. When the flame was applied to
the underside, good Lord the horde that
would fill the kitchen with salivation and an-
ticipation. Families face to face without dis-
traction, communing over the background
cries of sizzling onions and homemade fries.
There's glory there, back behind the canned
peaches if one just reaches. And below,
covered with pans of Teflon and aluminum
resides the cast-iron icon of a bygone era,
waiting to remind. Now light the ritual fire
and ignite memories of a simpler day: Mom
at home, kids with bibs, cantankerous sibs
and food the really did stick to your ribs.

HDTV

High definition television, just in time to re-
veal to us the true color of things. Blacks are
blacker, whites are whiter and an infinite
gradation between. Is this good? Maybe.
Too much information, differentiation, defini-
tion? Perhaps. Will we long for the gray-scale
of I Love Lucy? Some will. Have we moved
beyond the limitations of black and white?
It takes time for new technologies to gain
acceptance. Maybe we should discard the
notion of a color-blind society for one that
embraces the full spectrum.

In The Day

Hammer, nail, washboard, pail, all but white out of sight. The simple life, the good old days. AM radio, kick-the-can, Shirley Temple's dimple, life was so naively simple in the day. To the back of the bus without a fuss, divinely ordered races with plenty of open spaces. Ten cent movies, smoking in the balcony, garter belts and teacher's welts, all utterly sublime in its time. To be told to do and do it. Comfortable and secure in who you were and who you are. All the rights in your pocket and no court to knock it. Times were good in the day. All those others will have their days, if they are patient and mind their ways. While you're waiting your inalienable rights, may I offer you a slice of home-made chocolate cake and a glass of cold milk? Please sit right there on the back yard stoop.

In Heaven

In heaven there will be diamonds to wear, songs to sing, clouds to walk on, with musical accompaniment to it all. Nothing will be small. All pleasures and delights will be maximized. There will be eternal bliss without bliss-boredom. Each successive ecstasy will be a level above the previous on into mind-blowing eternity. Given this place of real whipped cream and home-made chocolate-chip cookies, will prayer really be necessary? What's to pray for when you have it all. What's to confess when you are without sin. Will it be necessary to attend church on Sunday? What for? Given the circumstances, what would the Preacher possibly have to preach about? Except maybe: "Sorry folks, because you've all been so darned good, once again the Sunday church service has been canceled."

Lindsey

Go back, go back to three so we can see
our little girl's smile again. Go back, go back
to five, so we can drive those warm glisten-
ing tears away. Go back, go back to ten
and remember how we loved you then, and
so love you here and now. Go on ahead
then, we know you must. We'll wait right
here and we trust, you'll not forget the tears
we dried, or the tears we cried.

Lauren

Come sit with me at three and feel the sun, my love and me. Know my heart is yours, know your love is my life. Know how beautiful you are. Sit with me at three and smile at me, that beam outplays the sun, and warms when that star cannot be seen. You shine so, I love you so.Come sit with me at three, see my hope that your tomorrow will be sweet and warm and bright. And in those days far from now, remember me as we sat together at three, and I was warmed by you and you by me.

Ruth

Ruth in her ninety sixth year no wrinkles appear. In reflection what's seen is a timeless sixteen. All blushing cheeks, fluttering lashes, behind rose-colored glasses. That this image persists despite the ravages of time is a miracle of a kind equal to or greater than any of the human mind. She had the ability in life to be both here and there at the same time. And so in death, Ruth remains both here with us in memory, and there —an eternal reflection of loveliness.

On Silence

What's there to say when nothing can be said? Speak the unspeakable? Silence is awkward, so go ahead say what can't be said in an insightful compassionate way. A derelict riding the rails dozes to the rock and clack in a tormented half-sleep, sprawled in an empty moving car. Be there too, with him in that rocking room. There's you and me and everyman and he. About his plight nothing can be said that will help him in any way. Yet we cannot resist preaching, confessing, advising, proselytizing. That man's never fully wakes in the room that shakes, carrying him down the line to the end of time and back again. What more can we say when there's nothing that can be said, and everyone is talking?

Soft Lens

You can smell his feet from one hundred yards away. A week's worth of skid marks on his drawers. Nose hairs and beard combine to filter cheap wine. With a crooked yellow grin, he's a most earthy fellow. He longs to be looked at, but never looks at himself. He knows that in the right light, with the right lens, at a particular angle he could be the him he might have been — the one no one can see, the one that can never be, yet exists in the last small room still occupied in the flop-house of his mind.

Skein

She speaks to her, she responds in overlapping lines. Back and forth they weave a tapestry of conversation. This verbal needlework work is rich in color and intricate in design. So complex are the layers that to any male listener the messages that pass are undecipherable. The finished product? There is none, the work is open ended. As the weavers depart, long twisted threads trail behind them.

The Girl With No Curl

She is delicate, faded amber in color and
intense. There are two notebooks in front of
her: a writing tablet and an Apple lap-top.
The pad is filled with characters as small
and precise as she. Once transcribed, the
computer will liberate those tiny symbols into
grandiose schemes and intricate designs
over which she will have total mastery. She
is attractive in a way that harbors no fool-
ishness, no errant course, no doubt of suc-
cess. She now ignores her work and turns to
People magazine in a self-conscious display
of eclecticism. I find her display authentic.
There is probably nothing she can't do ex-
cept be an overweight high school drop out
with three kids stuffed in a shopping cart at
Walmart, her hands filled with food stamps
and snot. She could not nor would not be
that girl. But can she understand that girls
plight? Can she empathize with her? Why
of course she can, it's all right there in those
little meticulously rendered characters wait-
ing to be digitized into an austere formulae
for summoning compassion and avoiding
failure.

What Matters

Size matters, fat matters, toothlessness mat-
ters. Color matters, ethnicity matters, your
car matters, your clothes matter. Every
single element of your appearance matters.
And anyone who tells you differently ... even
if that person happens to be an overweight,
toothless, albino Tutsi little person, dressed
in tatters, and driving a 1980 Toyota pickup
with bald tires. He, maybe more than most,
matters too.

The Facts

Where are the statistics on the war? The gory details, all of them. Football, baseball, basketball — arcane facts and stats rain down like an unending mortar barrage . On the financial page, analysis of every of market gasp, groan, retreat or advance. Charts, graphs, plans, tendencies and projections abound as ubiquitous as IUDs craters and craters soon to be in an Iraqi highway. Detailed details of the details. Where are those same details on the war? It's the information age, we love detailed analysis. Where are the details on the war? An in depth stat-sheet — The Carnage Street Journal. Numbers at least as important as batting averages or stock quotes. Where are the statistics on the war? Lost legs, left legs, right legs, both legs, fingers and arms, smiles, innocence, testicles, erections only in memory. All this broken down by age, sex, religion, bra size, shoe size. Faces erased, arms lost to girls between the ages of ten to fifteen, pregnant women killed and at what stage of pregnancy. The unborn not born, virgins deflowered, phalluses impregnated with steel, homeruns never hit, touchdowns never made. And the cost of the war per appendage. A $30,000 hand, a $120,000 pair of feet. Grief, quantify the grief, its depth, breadth and duration. Analyze it, weigh it, juxtapose I with laughter. The minutia too, a tongue here, a nasal membrane there. Where are the details on the war? Where are these analyses, the salient facts of life and death, the exploded view: All – the - parts – in - separate – sandy – places . Show – us – the – exploded – view, and – too – the – instructions – for – reassembly. Where are those stats sport fans? It's all there but no one cares to harvest, sort and know. The very reason for this savagery? To preserve our inalienable right to ignore. Our real passion is reserved for Stars, big cars and the Super Bowl. So a tank of gas costs a life, well hell cowboy, filler up! "You don't know? I thought everybody knew, A-Rod's battering 342."

***

Through the Looking Glass

In the window I sit, looking over my coffee cup and through a parkway pruned magnolia tree. Traffic wizzes by, a stiff clean breeze sways the trees as a lady in pink crosses from here to there. Cars in white turn left, cars in red turn right and the signal is always changing. Traffic cones restrict a south-bound lane as images, including that of me, are reflected in the mirror façade of the building opposite. A lady in black with a yellow umbrella avoids the sun but not the wind. Latinas pass by, I catch their eye. I smile, they deny. A young man crosses with ear-phones and clothes to fit a man three times his size. His head boobs to an unheard beat, his clothes randomly flap. A rumpled old man peddles by on a bike easily as old as he. Too fast, too slow, caution, stop and go. That's life moving at this moment, here, on this day, framed in the window of a corner cafe.

Why

Why does grass grow? I know science has an answer, but I don't believe it. You're telling me that a miniscule dot of who knows what exploded fifteen billion years ago and the result is growing grass? I don't believe it. There is something else going on there. You say you and me crawled out from the sea? I don't believe that either. I'll give you the earth's not flat, I'll give you that. But, that passion is chemistry — no way. Why there are masses and grasses is a mystery. Life itself is a mystery. All mysteries are one mystery.

—IMPORTANT NOTICE —

The One Mystery is available to you for a special low price of $20. (Please, cash only.) Hurry! The One Mystery is only available for a limited time and is not available any place else. The quantity is limit too, so act now. Once The One Mystery is gone, there will be no other mysteries.

That's it, 99 cents worth. Oh yea, you did give me a dollar, and you want change? You don't want change, you want your money back? You're kidding. You're not kidding? All right, all right, here's your god-damned dollar back. Live it up. You know my friend, you can't buy shit with a dollar!

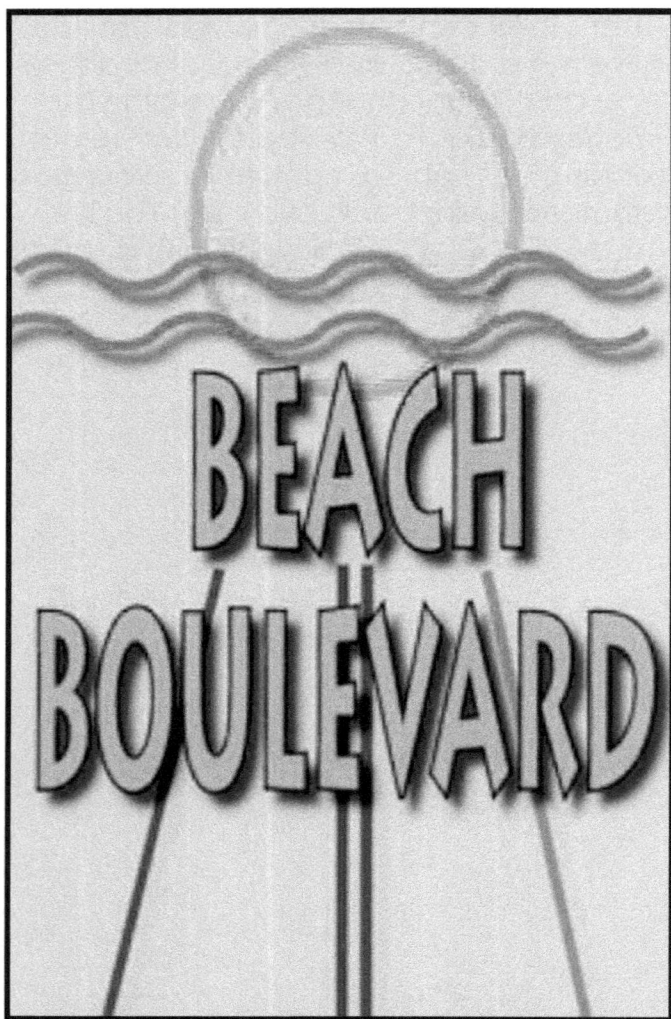

Beach Boulevard

It begins at Whittier Boulevard, and ends
twenty miles later at PCH. Pedestrians have
no chance here, an obstruction to the fits,
starts and coconut oil. The quintessential
Southern California artery where real blood
flows, 18" wheels smoke, forty is ancient,
in life and architecture and neither gets
respect. It is Beach Boulevard. On any day:
The Mother Hass avocado tree propels —
past endless fast food spots, service stations,
strip-malls, Knott's and Berry Farms, Disney
Lands, Tiger Woods phenomenons, and
Crystal Cathedrals. Down, down, down
to self-proclaimed North Shore wantabe
— Huntington Beach. Spilling out onto the
Highway of the Stars, surfboards sticking out
of cars, beautiful young girls, far too young,
far too beautiful, far too many from Malibu
to San Clemente.
On any day:
I'll prepare my way: shit, shower, shave,
brave the front page, turn to sports, then
leave the room. Tooling down the Highway
39, to where the paychecks grow. Buckled
down, slumped up, make the obligatory
motions. Pressed a button, and guess what,
the garage door opened again. Fed, bred,
said nothing of importance. Watched my
similes grow like the improbabilities of politics.
Hit the stairs, said no prayers, and undressed
my high school sweetheart — Evangeline, for
the 11,764th time.

On any day:

Four lanes stopped to the left of us. Four lanes stopped to the right of us. The Armies impatiently paused, the WALK signal flashes and off the curb steps an old dude, ear-budded, head down, cane working the blacktop. No way is this guy going to make it across before the General give the order to Charge! Is today the day he dies? Is today the day I have to watch him die? The insurgent makes his way, the vanguards turn their heads away. Our man crossing the valley of death, his thoughts are not on the danger of this trek, but on earlier times when he passed this way with wine and girls and endless dreams of endlessly balling every one of those endlessly beautiful girls with his endlessly erected erection. Well, old dude, that has ended, and you will be ended too, if you're not more wary of Beach Boulevard. When the Green light was given — thankfully, the outside columns were alert to the creeping menace and throttled back to let him pass. No wheels, entrails or puppy-dog tails — on the pavement, not right now. The intrepid urban adventurer survived another crossing. His dream never interrupted from curb to curb. "Look how beautiful she is here next to me. Dare I .... dare I.... touch that dimpled knee?"

On any day:
I stop and go with my turbo disengaged. The guy next to me's in a Corolla, been at my side since Imperial Highway. Waiting for the turbo to kick in, bo⁻h waiting for the turbo to kick in. I idle like few can idle, tap the pedal to growl at the competition, the envy is palpable. Get me to the beach parking lot, these things are so easy to park, costs no more to park a 150k Porsche than a 15k Corolla! I call it seashore equality.

On any day:
There, on the left, right there is the bus-stop where two old ladies waiting for Bus # 84, were finalized by a drunk 16 year old, driving an '69 Chevy milk truck. No milk inside, only empty beer cans and a boogy board. He got 2 years probation, and no remorse. The two old ladies lost a total of $14 on their unused transit passes, and got no frequent flyer miles for their flight from bench, to blacktop oblivion. This bisexual boulevard's a bitch. It's all like that, what I just described and more. Along this Boulevard, where the avocados, limes, Michelins, and Tequila bottles roll inexorably toward the sea.

On a past day:
There's a storefront just past Westminster Boulevard where they used to sell cigarettes cheap. That's about all they sold — smokes. How very sweet, my mentholated trip to the sea would be. Soothing, cruising dragging

down, between the smooth seashore-brown legs of baby oiled bleached hair Salemites. Inside the little store sat a little lady, as old as the sea, with the cough of a seal — ever puffing, and promoting smokers' rights. She was robbed continuously. There was the notorious Phillip Morris — a regular in these parts, and The Marlboro Man, spurs and all, easily identifiable by his distinctive hack. Even men of high station could not resist the plunder: Viceroys, Parliamentarians, even Lord Chesterfield was culpable. None of these felons, who, as you can see, came in all shapes, sizes and disguises, ever spent a day in jail — not a single fucking day! I stopped smoking, and the old gal stopped living. Those banditos still ride the Boulevard, now disguised in body art and nicotine patches.

On any Sunday:
It's a Sabbath morning in February, and it's raining all up and down Beach Boulevard. Every last inch of its black, white lined surface shines. The distillate, all of it, racing down Highway 39, in a futile attempt to dilute the sea. Those that spent 10 bucks for a carwash yesterday — well, hell man, it's got to rain in So Cal sometime. The Sunday parade up and down the great black way will have plenty of interruptions for slipping, sliding, and kissing body parts, followed by trips to the body shop for $2000 bumpers. Stay home today, read and write, try to get

it right. No way! That's bullshit I say! OK, OK, my Boulevard, I'm coming, I'm on my way, sideways if I must. What can I say, they have lined and paved the way.

On any day:
The smell of fresh cinnamon rolls at the corner of Manchester and Beach Blvd, about 11pm, gotta have one of them. Every size, shape and mood of my species, coming and going in glazed, crazed sugar-coated array. Running toward, fleeing away, on The Boulevard of never-ever-reach-dying-trying. Then in the end, the sandy life-sapping tide seething from beneath the sea. Blinding, binding blacktop road to a cul-de-sac'd burger joint. Life guard towers in asphalt bowers. Diminutive Latinas in long parades of progeny — in wheel chairs, strollers and serapes, crossing borders, babies slung. Alto! Amarillo! Prisa! Back and forth, you make it, again and again, most of you a la autopista treinta-nueve. Siete-Once — shop me and rob you. 3 pound burritos y super-size the fries — a la muerte! (All covered with processed cheese.)

On any day:
There's a vein of joy, right down the middle of Beach Boulevard. A dream line, double line, a straight line, an emerald line, to beach umbrellas and bronzed hope. A footbath for calloused feet, relief from the

endless heat, of never quite belonging, and longing to be home. Unwinding down to the shore via a magic black-top carpet; You can't get lost, Senora — just cross the horizontal line then follow the vertical ones. When the line ends, what then? You never know. There's always Hotdog stands and Life Guard Stands waiting for mouths that need resuscitation.

On any day:
On the boulevard, we run it to the sea with high revs, high riders, low riders, 75k SUVs, and giant pickups that have no room for freight. Propelled to the simple, endless panorama of the sand. Howling, trying not to understand, feeling carelessly simple. Briny sea-soft salve protects from that far off place beyond control, with its primal rays and blue viscous bays. Total emptiness of concern. Why the land lines hanging there? It's all invisible crisscrossing the air, wavelengths and right turns everywhere, the electromagnetic life is the only life we heed. Flat barking cats, mutilated purring dogs. STOP! you fucking moron. Dressed to kill in dream cars driven by 60 year old faces that would blow off if the top to that 500SL were down. Taunt, nerve damage stare, ever straight ahead. $5 a gallon gas. $5 an hour jobs No stores to rob. No green in the till. Let's drive by and shoot a homie. Nobody uses cash any more.

On any day:
Idling with the pack. Ford, Toyota, Volvo, BMW, Chevy Suburban and others. I remove my car from the pack — in mind, and the idling continues as my line moves up 25 feet. Straight ahead. Think not they, about the missing me? Oops, the pack is on the move. If I just had a Porsche Turbo to give me some status in the pack. An inimitable growl to penetrate the base response of those guzzling beasts. Stay forever in 2nd gear and redline often. Scream! Shout out! "Hey, you pathetic motherfuckers, it's me! I'm the one in lane one. I'm the fastest one, in the fastest thing."

On any day:
Try riding a bicycle along Highway 39, anywhere along Highway 39, you don't stand a chance! You just don't belong, and they tell you so, by voice, gesture, physical intimidation, and manslaughter. It all belongs to them, no one else is welcome: no bicycles, motorcycles, pedestrians, nothing that doesn't fit the four wheel description. Sure, they all hate each other, but their aversion to anything non-quadrupedal knows no bounds. Not only, they rightly believe, was Beach Boulevard build for the exclusive use of the automobile, the whole of Southern California was too. In all things, the mantra is: *Make it Driver Friendly.*

On any day:
Along the narrow center divider extending
out from a very busy intersection, is planted
a single row of Lilies of the Field. There,
against overwhelming odds, these urbanized
immigrants cling to life — even manage
a flower or two. Blown to, then fro, then
fro and to — traffic whizzes in opposite
directions on either side. When the light
changes to red, the real indignity begins.
The bombardment by cigarette butts, cold
coffee, used condoms, expectorant and
the like. Not an easy life to lead, here in
the city, for those of the field. "Who's idea
was it to plant us in such a place?" They
manage a smile once in a while, between
breaths of carbon monoxide. "Look out,
a lit butt! Mother fucking smokers! "Duck!,
here comes a beer can! Mother Fucking
alcoholics!" And oh God, the expletives, and
oh God, the base responses. We pray that
someday, in some way, one of my seeds will
get trapped in a tire tread, and end up in
the countryside. There, at least one of my
progeny will have a chance to become, in
fact, a genuine, down-home, shit-kickin, hell-
fire, authentic All-American Lily of the Field.

On any Day:
The blacktop is not acting. The gasoline is
not acting. That 2004 Toyota Camry is not
acting. Only the actor is acting. The greased
up fat lady in the beach chair is not acting
— had she been an actor, she wouldn't

have taken a part with no lines to speak.
The sixteen year old blond with a body like
climbing, twisting smoke — she is acting,
because she thinks she *has* to. She *has* lines,
but none to speak. None the less, she steals
the show.

On this particular day:
Truckin it down, shif-in it down, smoking
it down 39. Young girls below, dressed
naked. Diesel smoke, pants poke, bathe on
occasion — no truck stops down 39. Pedal to
the metal, right across PCH into the Pacific,
26 miles, and up in the middle of the Avalon
ballroom. I'll have a Bud please. None of
that light shit. Care to dance sweetheart?
Ya know, little gal, i-'s a long way home, and
salt water's no friend to my Peterbuilt.

On one particular day:
Here! Right here! At Talbert, in the back of
that liquor store. That's where the 13 year
old girl was raped, stabbed to death and
thrown in a dumpster. Pull in behind. I'll bet
that's the dumpster — right there. Stop. Let
me look. Sure, that's the one. Yea, I'll bet
this is the very one, I think I see dried blood
in there. Maybe a young girl's dried blood.
She was probably heading for PCH. Never
made it, Poor little thing. God damned
Highway 39 — and all the meth, cheap wine,
corkscrewed cocks, and twisted minds.
Fucking perverts everywhere! Did you see
that dried blood in there?

On any day:
From end to end, I spend a lifetime on
Beach Boulevard, and 10,000 gallons of gas
an hour. Often motionless, waiting, waiting
for the signal to proceed. Foreshortened, it's
a cacophony of flashing amber, red and
green lights — honk, honk, fender-bender life
ender, exhaustive pent up anger. Opaque
window glass all enabling anonymity, the
architecture of Dubai.

On one particular day:
The highway to the seaside is packed with
lovers and their songs, in various stages of
rapture. Lips press lips, as at least one set of
eyes strains to watch the little white lines.
Simultaneously, a young Latino, with a green
bandana across his face, reaches across
the counter of Lucky's Liquor Store, and
splits open the head of Mama-san — west to
east. He takes a carton of Salems, a quart
of Tequila and $311 dollars, while deftly
avoiding an expanding pool of blood. The
bandito then mounts his '72 Mustang and
heads down the dusty road, falling in behind
all the others, seeking songs with a Latin
beat, the press of blood-red lips, precipitous
cleavage, and someone to share his of
machismo with. He is, this handsome young
caballero, a real authentic lady killer.

On any day:
An ocean view. A home with no ocean view. Very desirable to most and beyond reach for most. Usually, what's seen for the substantial premium is a far off, seldom distinguishable line between gray-blue sky, and gray-blue sea, that yields static views that seldom provokes wonder, except when the mortgage payment is due. An urban view, now that's a whole other matter. From my loft, I peer down upon an ever changing panorama of animation and strife. Gesticulations, blaring horns, gun fire pops, screaming sirens, trains, planes and automobiles all coliding before my eyes — accompanied by the thundering base response of darkened eyes, and too-cool bumpy rides. The tingle of shadowy figures lurking in the dark. Oh, sure, you'll get a red sail in the sunset on occasion, but compare this to a mid-summer-night's carjacking, followed by a high-speed police pursuit, shooting and bent metal and the sound of shattering glass and dreams. Not even in the same ballpark. Sell that mildewed peek-a-boo view of the Pacific for immersion in a real-time display of urban, dramatic, kinetic decay.

On any day:
A fish taco dog day, waves and radiating blacktop. Slight guilt creeps into the irresistible movement toward the shore. I arrive to realize this trip's to nowhere but

saltwater and sand. Simply seawater, sand
— science sans mystery. I sit there on a
cold gray day, looking down at the sand.
Nothing, absolutely nothing is revealed to
me. I am a liar. The hills — again, are all on
fire, and the sand slips unabated through my
feeble fingers. My soul is overcast, and smells
of dead fish and burning brush.

On any day:
A whimsical, impulsive act, (In mind, I'd
rehearsed it all before). Now, chance
and a joint-buzz coupled. Red light, in the
curb lane. Bus bench in my line of sight.
There sits a worn misused young beauty
smudged with urban soot, misused by
others, misused by herself. All in a two
second's gaze I have accessed a human
work of visual art needing restoration. And,
I know of an empty gilded cage in need
of occupancy. The traffic light is about
to change. I Roll the window down. Can
I give you a ride somewhere? *Sure, sure,*
she responded. Gathered up her plastic
bags and scrambled in. The signal turned
to green, better it had flashed red. Now
started, the play must go on. Where you
going doll? I asked with a slight quiver
in my voice. *Where you going doll?* was
her response. I'd like to do something for
you, a proposition if you will. *Ya baby, I do
propositions",* she interrupted. No, not like
that. I want to get you a place to stay for
a while, and fix you up a bit … like, see if

I can restore what I know is down below.
*Oh, like those TV makeover shows. Sloppy
fat bitch, into a made-up, well dressed
full-bodied bitch. You've got a camera
hidden somewhere, right?* No camera.
What's your name? *Your fuckin with me,
right?* No, no, nothing like that, Indulge me,
if you will. *My name is Emily, Emily Brand —
Branded, if you like.* I'll go with Emily, I like
that. We will make you an Emily again, or
maybe for the first time. We will brand you
— an Emily." Then, her lines not yet totally
devoid of grace, dirty nails, calloused feet,
a weary weathered face and yet unfaded
eyes of blue, she stepped with excitement
into my salon to restore the appearance
of elegance that was, or maybe wasn't,
once there. Meth, crack, pills and booze,
what about those? *I don't do any of that
shit any more, at least not right now.* I will,
she will, cheat the Boulevard of its meat,
at least for right now. It would take a while,
and a few bucks. It did take a while, and
more than a few bucks. Over time she was
scrubbed, rubbed, manicured, pedicured.
coiffured, and sandstoned. Saw doctor,
dentist and psychologist. Paring, peeling all
the grub away. Seeking the essence down
below. Always thinking I will love her then.
I know that when I get deep down under I
will love her then, what she looks like then.
Reprogramming of the whore-core? I don't
kid myself about that, and there's no way
in hell I can kid the real Emily Brand about

that. I promised myself not to fuck her until
at least some beauty had rubbed through,
and the lab reports came back. When I did,
she gave a good performance, I could not.
A vaginal gorge of National Park proportions
rendered me overmatched, and I'm not
into anal sex or fisting. All the questions
you would ask, I did not want answered:
How she got on the street, children, family
all the stuff that might explain the reason
for her plight. No facts please, they can
be devastating to illusion. All I want is the
appearance of beauty the appearance of
grace. A tranquil sea with mermaids and
dolphins beneath. Substance? what good is
substance? Substances got her on the street.
She indulged me, I indulged her. Beauty,
beast — each partly each. This lasted
maybe a month after the total renovation
was complete. Oh God, I loved the look
of her, the image of her, the picture I'd
painted of the idealized Emily. The canvas
was not complete, the Boulevard Emily was
not in it. I looked at her, and looked at her.
She seldom looked at me. She peers with
wonder at herself in the mirror. Most often,
she looked out the window, and down
the street — wanting repatriation. She was
now elegant in all ways, yet incomplete
without the street. The Brand wanted to be
complete. We stop at the corner of Beach
and McFadden. Red light, bus stop bench,
she got out. Long floating strides away.
Over her shoulder she looked back at me,

smiled and mouthed the words *I love you*. I
loved her looking back that way, and how
she looks, and her moving hips and lips—
the Emily, the appearance of Emily. Thus,
I released her back into the wild. The light
turned green, for the second time, and I
headed south toward PCH — broke, failed
and Branded. As fucked up as I was before,
now, maybe more.

On any day:
Sitting on the redwood decking of my
avocado tree shaded patio I look down
toward the sea. I can't see the sea, but
I know it's there just 20 miles down that
road. You know dude, it's all downhill
from here, to sand, then sea, then China,
and the Russian Steppes, to balls in the
sand and dried semen in the back seat.
Opacity receding from the skin, revealing
lines beneath the Boulevard: sewer lines,
utility lines, rat lines and cucarachas — all
telling each other: *It's all downhill from here
brother, it's all downhill from here.*

On any Day:
Heading back up Beach Boulevard about
6pm. Top down, shirt off —toasted white
bread, a beautiful young thing beside
me. An unbearably physical young thing
bedside me. Can't keep my eyes off of
where those mocha thighs lead. There's a
throbbing in my ears. After idle chit-chat and
reinforcing glances, my hand finds a place

on her warm thigh. I wait ... an interminable
few seconds for sign of rejection, there was
none. I slide my hand up and feel her legs
lightly part. She is mine! She is warm and
moist, I am faint. She reaches over and
strokes the bulge beneath my gray-white
O'Neill board shorts. I am frantic, I've got to
find a place to pull over! Jesus Christ man,
this is a convertible. Yea, there's the closed
down Highway 39 Drive-In Theater. I pull in,
find a good spot near the concession stand
and park. She jumps on me, and we forget
about the movie, had there been one. Or
popcorn and cokes, had there been any. I
went so deep, and she was everything. The
late afternoon was all beauty in every way,
and the power of our lust was everything. Oh
dear God, can it get any better than this?
Pan back to: vacant drive-in theater, late
afternoon sun stretching, open convertible,
beautiful girl riding beautify boy. Pan further
back: that's Beach Boulevard there on
the right, with its stream of dreamers and
screamers. Look up — that's the ocean
there, pulling the sun down onto her, as I am
pulling ecstasy down upon me. Dear God,
on reflection, it never did get any better
than that. (For the Boulevard, Ocean, Sun,
and this sensuous girl — I cannot speak.)

On this day in October:
Santa Ana Canyon breaths deeply in, opens
her mouth, and exhales a scorching breath
across the plain and out to sea, sending with

it Summer's debris on an October visit to Catalina Island. 101 degrees of oven dry air sweep the land clean and ten million bad hair days ensue. And, just maybe, if Mother Haas allows eight foot surf with tops blown back. Wave faces standing up an extra two seconds, wavering. reluctant to pitch over, leaving their white caps streaming behind them in the in the arid off-shore wind. And while the sea plays epic Dick Dale, the Hills too rail, and trail back with white — as the brush ignites the harvest moon to ember glowing orange. I must travel down The Boulevard this day. No death or threat of alimony will keep my wheels from spinning down 39 to its end. Standing on the shore with Santa Anas pushing at my back and the sea in epic surge, I well up. No, there's no sand in my eye, it's the glory of it all. An epic Southern California day. So, maybe your house is on fire, but with barrels like these, who really g ves a shit. As God is my witness, it doesn't get much better than this — here and now at the very end of Beach Boulevard.

***

A Turkey's Lament

My mother told me I could be anything I wanted to be. I wanted to be ... a soaring eagle. My mother lied to me! Till the moment of my decapitation, I still believed, despite all evidence to the contrary. My head is fertilizer, my body lies before you. Who do I blame for this dream turned nightmare? I think I know why my mother lied to me, and I forgive her for that. I think I know why I lied to myself, and I can't forgive that. So, go ahead, pick my bones — enjoy! Apparently, I lived for this moment. God made eagles to fly, God made turkeys to die. But ... still, when the dishes are done, and my wish-bone's set out to dry, one truth lingers, like an eternal fire — my finely feathered mother was a liar.

Boy Talk

I watched the Padre sin on me. I felt the Padre sin on me. It felt good when the Padre sinned on me. The Padre said he loved me. I loved the Padre too. Later, the Padre killed himself. I am still here, wondering if, in that act, he once again sinned on me.

Angelina Dreaming

In a dream last night: I entered Angelina's
bedroom, a very big bedroom, and it was
all filled with mostly men, and some women
too. There was this spindle dispensing
numbers and everyone had to take a
number. There sure are lots of guys (and
Gals) who want to fuck Angelina, and to do
both speakable and unspeakable things to
her. My number was 987. I thought, given
these circumstances, whacking off in the
tool shed isn't all that bad. So, off I went (in
my dream) to the tool shed. Guess what,
there she was in the tool shed! I fucked her
brains out, on the work bench right next to
the grinder — a little worried she'd soil her
red silk nightgown on something like Elmer's
glue. Ya know what though, dried Elmer's
glue looks just like ... well, you know what.
Often do I hear *Oh Brad! Oh Brad! in her
writhing joy.* Pity all those others waiting in
the bedroom — all those other premature
ejaculators. After our simultaneous
cataclysmic eruption, I stood there eyeing
the power saw and those voluptuous lips,
then went in the house. Angelina could not
follow, that would never work. I keep that
little arrow-shaped piece of paper with #987
on it in the top right-hand drawer of my
dresser. My Speedos are in that drawer too.
I love Angelina. We visit often. In August,
at 110°, I lick the salt from her eyelids as
she cries out there beside my vise — in the
steaming outback-dream-shed.

Cored

There was this white pastoral chapel next to an apple tree in a green valley. The church had a steeple, but no people. the tree had presence, but just a single apple. The church just sat there hungering for soul food while the apple just hung there fearing freefall and decay. One particularly sensuous summer evening, that chapel ate that apple! Thus, an alliance was formed between the church and fresh fruit, spawning the Pectinarian movement. A basic tenet of Pectinarianism is this: There must be, at all times, some fresh fruit adorning every alter. That sect morphed into what we know today as the Episcopal Church — or, if you prefer your fruit imported, the Church of England. [Homophobic? I think not. Surely those as liberated as Episcopalians, will enjoy the this light-hearted jibe.

Cha-lu-pa

I am Cha-lu-pa. Strong against Cortez's
Sea, I love my name Chalupa. Chalupa!
Chalupa! Chalupa! There, on my bow is
Chalupa, written bold in Baja azure blue. The
Dorado know Chalupa, The Wahoo know
Chalupa, The great gray ballenas know me
too! They all shout to me: *Ola Cha-lu-pa!*
*Be safe, smile, bounce easily upon the sea
Chalupa! You, Chalupa, are one of us. You,
Chalupa, are one with The Sea. One day,
dear Chalupa, we will take you down to see
El Rey.*

Hawkeye

I was all set to kill myself in 2000; then ...*The Sopranos* came along. I had to put my plans on hold. Then ... *Six Feet Under* came along, and I was forced to admit life had, at least temporarily, some value. Now, they're both gone, and reruns don't do it for me. My life's now in your hands, HBO and NETLIX. Produce something compelling and diverting — or I die! The Sony remote rests in my hand like a limp dick awaiting arousal. Writer, directors, producers, actors — please join together and save me from the bathroom door wherein is stored the appliances of death: razors, pills, reflections, chronic diarrhea, and artless programming. Where have you gone Jerry Seinfeld? Rescue me Barney Fife! I was personally saved from death many times in the *Mash* field hospital tent. Man can't live by *Jeopardy* alone. I swear by macro-HD-images of primordial slime, I *will* commit the act of final deliverance this time, and pull that plug that has for so long sustained me.

Haute Cuisine

Never ever seek the truth, it is far too sharp a weapon to wield. Truth is: holding a child's hand on the stove to teach him about heat, and pain. Truth is, showing a loved one the twelve pieces of her beloved in the bottom corner of a body bag. Truth is, telling your wife of twenty-three years you've never been really happy, but have now found it, in the haute cuisine of an eighteen year pussy. Truth is: microbes, atoms, worms, rats, lies, politicians, movies stars, Las Vegas. diarrhea and dementia, and that's not all. Truth is not what's written here or anywhere. Truth is what you do, and what is done to you.

I am it

I consume to part the gloom. Mine's a
consuming passion for consumption —
ecological consumptionism: mine the pit,
slicken the sea, styrofoamate the landscape,
500 horsepower turds, indisposable
disposables, kidneys of blue where no
moisture's due. I confess to *it*, cannot
live without *it*. *It* is me, I am *it*. Without *it* I
deflate. I sit alone separate from my parts
with candlelight's glow, tic-tac-toe, solitaire
with dog-eared non-vinyl coated playing
cards. Please God, save my amenities:
food to go, with an inch of napkins, twenty-
seven packets of condiments all sheathed
in phthalated, polyvinyl chloridated
polystyrene — meant to outlast the planet
Mercury. Bind me up in plastic wrap, lie me
down in my sin. I am him — the consumer
of planets, he who orders super-sized solar
system fries.

Live With It

Veined hands try vainly to erase tears with
type-set symbols on glaring white paper.
Most of the time it works, concentrating
on what the hand is writing, and ignoring
the hand that writes. Brats want mommy,
mommies drive too fast, mommies fuck
too fast. Old folks drive too slowly, think too
slowly, and hardly fuck at all. Jeans too low,
revealing the tattooed split between youth
and forty-two. Jeans belted just below the
armpits and World War Two. It's all America
and a lot more too — live with it.

I can't wait to see.

Just outside the bar, she threw her head back against the brick wall and screamed. She was pregnant she said, and I didn't care! She was right. not in the head pounding, but in the fact I didn't care, not right now anyway. This tantrum shit was cutting into my drinking time. What do I do now? Couldn't she just cool it until about noon tomorrow, after I had splattered her with my remorse? This whole scene was so overtly theatrical to one seeking booze and not dramatic display. I panned back: Pretty young girl emoting. handsome, angular young man pleading, the neon bar sign flickering, the receding darkened street — the set. I've seen this all before, in a movie, but this is real, and I am in it. This beautiful, hysterical girl is in it. and there is a real fetus in it, and plenty of real tragedy too. This scene has it all. I can't wait to see the first cut.

Lost in Translation

No human being is responsible for the chaos in the Middle East in the past, the present or the future. It's all God's fault. He's the leader, we follow. Shame on you God, for misleading. We want to understand, but are unable to break your arcane code. What language does God speak anyway? Maybe the instructions are lost in translation. He speaks, we listen, translators write it down but misinterpret. Abraham got it wrong. Moses got it wrong. Jesus got it wrong. Mohammad got it wrong. Nobody, ever, has figured out what the hell the guy is talking about, and that's his fault, not ours. Dear God, make it simple. Keep it to ... say, three things. Thing One, Thing Two, and Thing Three. Can you handle that? I apologize for my impudence, but you've had a lot of time to work this out. Look, the aforementioned quartet got it wrong — right? You've got only one choice: If you want to get your message through, say exactly the same thing to everyone — individually, and dumb it down.

Japanese Zero

Thirty-something chick entwined with a patio
chair. Table and umbrella equally Asian.
Elbows in close, large coffee, sunglasses,
soft droopy hat, working a cigarette
between the wrong fingers, ear buds, and
a continuous cell phone conversation
that made you wonder if there really was
someone on the other end. Talk, sip; talk,
puff; talk, talk, talk. Legs wind, unwind,
wind like the rubber band in a model
plane. Say a Japanese Zero. She presents
an impenetrable silk veil to a lumbering
white western man. Now why in hell would I
attempt contact with her. She is so rice-bowl,
staccato, incommunicado. Unless you speak
the language. She is to me, inscrutable. Is
she attractive enough to overcome my fear
of the unknown? No way, she scares me to
death! She would bore into your soul and
suck the senses dry. You'd end up having to
bludgeon her to death and burying her in
the backyard, deep down, under the cherry
tree. I'd owe her mangled tangled body
that — all rooted in cherry trees, the Korean
peninsula, the Japanese archipelago, and
ancient Chinese rice paddies. May her
pieces rest in peace, along with ear buds,
entangled legs, Parliament cigarettes, and
the Transcontinental Railroad. I'll go alone
to Chinatown, and eat raw things from the
Sushi bar, and remember how frightened I
was —and how I dismembered my fear.

Make Way!

It's called a three wheel jogging stroller: brakes, pockets, baskets, cell phone holders, water bottle holders, all manner of dangling things, pneumatic tires, and — oh yes, a place for a kid, and I don't mean a baby goat. In it, for the moment, is a fifty pound four-year-old, with NASCAR approved crash-helmet and shoulder restraints. Strapped in, not for his safety, for the safety of those they encounter. After driving the more sedate to cover along their jogging route, the terrorists arrive at Starbucks. They enter, perambulator and all — God help our shins! Baby Huey wants this. Baby Huey can't have that. Baby Huey can't have that either. Baby Huey activates the siren. La Petite Mere, blonde pony-tail sticking through the back of her Dodger baseball cap, Mama Huey can't decide what combination of ingredients the alchemist should blend for her latte. Behind their obstruction to an orderly existence, the line serpentines out the door. Finally, the order is completed, and out that door they go. There is cheering, muted by most, but cheering none-the-less. How sweet our freedom is, how petty are the annoyances to that freedom.
Look out! OMG, I think they're coming back! Baby Huey spilled is his grande pumpkin spice decaf nonfat milk whipped cream topped latte all over their Bieshon Friese Pepe la Moco. Mama Huey goes right

to the front of the line demanding restitution. The line demands justice. As the situation starts to get as ugly as Baby Huey, I leave. Is this a great country or what?

***

Mary's Done

Two days out of port, it's clear to the crew
that my newly Shanghaied bride, is the
fourth member of a three party crew. That
crew being: the Captain — Me, D.R. (Demon
Rum), and Virgin Mary, the blond blue-eyed
nymph who spends all her time hanging out
over the bow. With nary a tinge of regret,
and an almost imperceptible hesitation, we
piped my new bride over the side, and into
a dingy — one nautical mile off the Santa
Monica Pier. Then he, the vaporous D.R.,
and me, the listing Captain, and she, the
Wooden Maiden, head out to sea, modestly
guilt-ridden at our treachery, but amply
stored with 100 proof consolation in the hold.
We sail south, beyond the hemisphere's ring,
bound to ride Drake's Passage in drunken,
fearless, suicidal play. Along the way,
we engage sea-farers large and small in
titillating repartee: gulls, flying fish, dolphins,
constellations, parts of the moon, all of the
moon, and all the parts of the dark that are
willing to chat, plus Stars and Mars, and the
fiery orator St. Elmo. I even thought to chat
with the multitudes below, but my darling
Mary dissuaded me on each occasion. My
dearest virgin figurehead, I have promised to
drive her deep into tempestuous exotic seas,
to let her ride the Horn, see the place where
the greatest Oceans meet, and drink deeply
of my cold, blue-green metaphors. Spirits,
Demons, and the Deep, commingled

illusions of Homeric proportions — an odyssey clearly shown to me in wasted briny hours. Finally, we managed the place where oceans and fates meet. The indignant rolling seas, immediately demand our presence below — Davey's become impatient. First, my Liege, let us ride awhile, I promised the young lady? Our stay granted, immediately I abandoned the wheel, and mounted my Mary's substantial oaken ass, pounded in the belaying pin, reached around and held tightly to her hardened slippery breasts. Never before had she made a sound, but in those moments, I am absolutely sure, (as sure as a drunken sailor can be), there came from those chiseled red lips a gasp, followed thereafter by a groan. Oh dear God! we all rode like Hell. Over and over again, defiantly, she and he and me, penetrated deep into the rolling waves, plunging deep, rising high, plunging deeper, rising higher — unimagined glimpses of eternities, and foaming sprays of ecstasies. In this rage of sea, indecency and maiden's blood, Phlegyas appeared and took the abandoned helm. *"You'll do well below, he assured, "I've come to steer you down"*. We were satisfied that it was time to see how eternal damnation might be, so down we went — deep, deep down — down where darkness cannot see, down where memories cannot recall. Down 1000 fathoms below the pilings of the Santa Monica Pier where, at certain times, on certain nights, when the moon be right, a dingy can be seen bobbing there — empty, save a sodden wedding veil, the sole remnant of this equally sodden tale.

***

Residential Area

Plan me, incorporate me — spread me out
and plat me. Lay out my erogenous zones,
detail ingress and egress, high traffic zones,
dead ends streets, dangerous intersections,
where to park, where not to park. Decrease
Speed, enjoy the view. Increase Speed,
almost home. Plan my community, make
me easily accessible, a perfectly ordered
neighborhood. Make me user friendly. Cul-
de-sac me. Map my moods. Indicate the
dream fields, and the pot fields. Now, let
me see the map you've drawn. Well done!
So, you are here, and ... you want to go
where ... exactly? Oh yes, I concur that route
will get you there. Let's stop often along the
way. I'm so, so eager to begin. Sin? Oh, yes,
ample sin has been figured in.

Dad

Dad was a hero. He was able to leap tall buildings with a single bound. Really. He was absolutely anything I wanted him to be. Dad would do anything for me. Often, he would take me along on his jaunts in the pursuit of truth and justice. Softly, his arm of steel would gather me to his hip and we'd fly very high and very fast till my breath was nearly taken away. Excitement surely few have known. He's gone now, leaving me to face the lawless on my own. I'm not as good at it as he was, Gosh, I can't even fly. Not a day goes I don't heave a deep sigh thinking of the softness of his steely grip and the warmth of his righteous grin.

Same train, same seat

Through the window, commuter trains come,
stop and go. Often, I see the same people
on the same train, in the same seat, at the
same time every day. I wonder if one of
those same riders ever gets off the train at
all — has been dead for years and nobody's
noticed. That same rider celebrates every
holiday in the same way — motionless in
the sitting position. I'm going to buy a ticket
on that train and sit right down next to the
guy and see for myself. Maybe I'll start a
conversation, or even a friendship with this
fellow, vital signs or no. Hell. it just might be
fun. Then some other voyeur might see two
figures side-by-side. on the same seats, in the
same seats, at the same time every day
and wonder if they are lovers — the cadaver
and me.

Spanish Revival

New communities laid out like graph paper, clean, regulated, cul-de-saced, yet minds set free from old restraints, and sullied reputations. How sweet it is here: palm trees, San Diego red bougainvillea, lawns with sprinklers systems, fuchsias, swimming pools little rain, and simultaneously riding snow and surf. Two plus cars, two plus bathrooms, drive-in salvation. Wheels, it's all about the wheels. Tear up the tracks, widen the roads, right-of-ways, more right-of-ways. Pedal to the metal and the ever blooming rose. Igor Stravinsky, me, and Gregory Peck, shoulder to shoulder at the Farmers Market. All so sweet then, so sweet now. The actors have changed, and multiplied with pixilation's added parts. The demographics of Santa Monica, Laguna Beach, and all in-between have changed, still the Golden Age lingers, still there's a thrill to it all. It may be hard to conceive of Malibu down to San Clemente as my hometown? But goddamn it, I do!

The Grin on Jimmy Hendrix's Face

My dear Mozart, you too JS Bach, and
Tchaikovsky, Beethoven, Liszt, Ravel, Berlioz
— all you guys,what have you written lately?
What you have done is admirable, but how
many times can we be expected to listen
to a D minor Mass, 5th Symphony, Magic
Flute, Bolero, et. al., and still give it the
attention we are told, and tell ourselves, it
deserves? There is so much that is new and
exciting out there, don't you fear losing your
base? I mean, same old ensembles, same
old instruments, same old instrumentalists,
same hairy gyrating batons. Do you have
any idea of how much talent is out there
now, and the resources they have to make
music with? If you did, and given your past
achievements, you'd be right up there on
the charts. Is it a management problems?
Stratification? Hey Wolfy, get your hands
on an electric guitar, and rent some digital
studio time. I can see the grin on Jimmy
Hendrix's face now. One promise, and
this applies to all of you guys — don't get
nostalgic and go acoustic on us!

The Morning before

On a day not too far from now that will
never ever arrive, a vote is taken. (All the
world is democratized, and every single
being votes.) To be, or not to be, was the
question before the electorate — A yes or
no vote on this: Everyone in the world has
everything they ever wanted and everyone
is miserable, should we go on? The vote
was taken and the "I just can't go ons won."
Now how to exterminate the minority, those
who voted to carry on. The Majority took a
vote among themselves and decided in this
democratic way to: Fuck the minority! The
approved elixir was rancid California wine
mixed Florida swap water. And the wake
began to put the human race to sleep for
good. Some party it was. There was all those
willing drinkers, and about 2.5 billion non-
willing drinkers. Oh God, I can't even begin
to tell you about the shit that went on. The
minority was finally subdued, and the wine-
coolers imbibed. I worked, it really worked!
Now everybody wanted nothing and got
it. Not a single dissenting voice. No popcorn
breath. No drudgery. No Big Mac attacks.
No rationality. Oh sure, dogs still chased cats,
and all that stuff but, things were different.
Quiet. Only essential sound was heard.
Beethoven's Ninth was never played again.
All the squirrels and similar rodents agreed,
this was a good thing, that tune had been
heard enough!

To Be A Poet

The quality of what is being produced in the name of poetry these days is deep, deep beneath the standard of sub-standard. More disturbing still, these word arrangements and syntactical abominations are being labeled *Poetry* by their authors. Standards must be set, and qualifications met, for who does and doesn't have the right to call themselves A *Poet*, and what does and what doesn't qualify as *Poetry*! I can be of assistance in those determinations. To be entitled to the appellation *Poet*, the supplicant must:
—Have at least a Master's Degree from a University that actually has classrooms, degreed instructors, and requires your physical attendance, in person, on a regular basis
—Have published two *things* and have one *thing* in the works.
—Abhor rhyming.
—Do monotone readings of his irrational ramblings to gatherings of monotones.
—Call himself A Poet without a blush, either externally or internally. As to what qualifies to be called *A Poem*: Any of the works produced by a writer who has qualified as *A Poet*. All other non-qualified writings, heretofore claiming the status of poetry, shall fall under the heading of Quasi-*poetry*, and shall be called such. Those writing *Quasi-poetry* shall be called *Quasi-poets* (QPs).

QPs may achieve the status of *True Poet* (TP) by meeting the *True Poet criteria*, as set forth here. In case you're wondering, I am a *QP*. How is it a *QP* sets the standards for *True Poetry*? How is it cowards send brave young men off to die? A paradox? Yes, it's a paradox to die for another's lie. Paradox is a great word, and I'd love to go into why, but I must *qualify and that leaves* time for little else. You see: I am teaching, pursuing a Master's Degree, working on two books at once, have another in outline form, and frequently do readings of my works to my children at bedtime. And, late at night, looking into the bathroom mirror, I repeat over and over again: "I am a poet! I am a poet!" The external blush I have nearly under control; internally though, pesky doubt pervades. So, what have you learned from this encounter with me? Yes, I have lofty aspirations, that's true. Anything else? *You're full of shit?* Yes, like anyone, I am, at times, full of shit. That will pass. Anything else? No, I'm not too old to dream. The real problems is not my dreams, but remembering them! That's a joke ... of course. Anything else? No. You have to leave. Well, thanks for stopping by, do so anytime. Maybe next time, I'll be *a Poet!* Or the time after the time after the time after that. You don't think so? I wasn't aware you did much of that — reading or thinking I mean. No, fuck you! *Fuck who?* No, I regret to say, my mother's long dead! Killed by a runaway Semi. (Semi-Sonneteer).

***

The Extended Arm

Perfectly darling 24 year old young woman pushing a stroller containing a perfectly beautiful 18 month old little girl circumvents the extended arms and steps into the path of the southbound Metrolink. She had a chance. The engineer and the baby didn't. Nothing anyone would want to see. Nothing anyone would want to hear. But, it was the truth that day. The screeching, mangled, entangled truth that day. Had you been a witness to this tragedy, your life might not have changed much, but your dreams forever would.

About

I am a bird.
Never mind what kind.
I'm not sure myself.
Anyway, I fly here there
and everywhere.
I love the view from above,
being above it all, almost.
I'm a very happy bird.
Watching me fluttering about,
can you harbor any doubt?

ZIGZAG#1

The sign says: THE BUS STOPS HERE.
Am I expected to believe that?

At the bus stop, Virtuous Perpetua waits
patiently for a streetcar. The tracks were
torn up 50 years ago.

City bus Zigzag #1 from Union Station
to every where, serpentines through LA,
stopping here, there and Pershing Square,
Bunker Hill, MacArthur Park, the Coli-
seum, Chinatown, Hollywood and the
Santa Monica Pier. Riders on and off as
is their way. Some you've heard of, most
you haven't. Veterans of wars and life,
scattered along the route, on benches,
sidewalks, in the leaves of grass. Many
huddled in smoke-free cubicles obscured
behind tinted window glass that further
grays their day, while they expand from
munching energy bars, and the unearthly
stress of tech support from Mars. No
mystical, mythical transport this. Neither
subway, elevated rail, or bullet train —
simply a rocking, hissing, smoke belching,
non-articulating blue whale, gathering in
and spilling out indigestible pray along the
way, as it plies the murky mist that engulfs
LA. No fuss, just a generic bus. Get on,
sit down, stand up, get off. I live a very
comfortably on the West Bank of the LA
River, in the roomiest of enclosures, that
once housed a 36" Westinghouse side-by-

side stainless steel refrigerator. Thank God
for the middle class affliction with consump-
tion. From LA's Seine, conduit for tumble
weed, wine bottles, and the arid Santa Ana
wind that channels city soot to the sea, I
meander over to Union Station, from where
my circuitous daily ride begins. Aboard
Zigzag #1, we have regular riders, irregular
riders, and frequently a few surprisers. All
along the way, I make copious notes in my
little journal with a stubbed down pencil
that works great for cramped spaces and
for under-sharpened urban insights. When
boarding Zero-Zero-One, I get, if I can, a
side-facing seat so I may take in the entire
panorama of figures and faces; allowing
me to pencil in the shadows they cast
onto the pages of my little unlined book,
with minimal obstruction to my angular
view of who they are, and what they do.
Passing endless walls of tagged concrete,
parallel and horizontal people, I breathe
in the wrecking ball dust of LA's history.
Fields of lined asphalt, earthquake oblivious
buildings, glass-faced, with no windows
that can be flung open. It's near impossible
to jump out of a high-rise when the
windows have no crank or latch, just tinted
impenetrable double-paned self-reflection.
Parking structures are a good bet for
unassisted flight. Go directly from the
driver's seat over the railing, to the street.
Freeway fly-overs are even more efficient
in ending despair. You only die once —
right? Then do it right! A fifty foot drop, an

abrupt landing in lane one and you're done! Too sweet. Disposed of by cerebral gridlock, gravity, and a Caltrans street-sweeper. There was history in this town, but we tore it all down. Pitted against SoCal land values, history has no chance. There are blue-velvet Galleries, and Cathedrals with their dark apses for ecclesiastical lapses, and architecture at oblique angles to separate itself from what went before. Sidewalk cafes in some places, a bookstore or two. But it all seems pretentious, our tanned attempt at sophistication in shorts and flip-flops. We squint our eyes and halfheartedly pretend *to be*. We do a lot of pretending *to be* — that's the fun of it all. Mostly, we have sunshine and automobiles, all amped- up by double shots of tequila, tightly wrapped young asses and the taunt smiles of overly lifted faces. The movies? Those too. And the people that are in those movies, and the people that make those movies. Malibu, Brentwood and Bel Air's where they live. This particular bus doesn't stop in those particular places. There are buses that go there, and stop there, but you can't get off there. Better all-around that way. Besides, there is no urban glory like the glory of 5th Street. No manicured lawns or ostentatious attempts at urbanity — just mob-scene casting calls, fizzling hope, and wine in bottles with twist-top caps for a one dollar high. My pencil would not get stubby haunting the environs of Brentwood or Malibu (OJ notwithstanding).

Watts Towers shadow Eiffel Towers, and
more relevant art on cinderblock walls
than suspended in the Louvre. The City of
Lights is no match for the muzzle flashes
of Lincoln Heights. Yo dog, you from this
neighborhood? The Main Library steps
reach out to me as we pass, but I can't
make myself go in there, unless it's to take
a piss. Dusty books and musty people
scattered about. My refined senses object
to that. Better the bathed-in-after-shaved
me, on the bus looking out at the temple
stairs. I don't suppose the books resent
sharing their space with puffy-eyed dozers,
at least the furniture and the toilets get
used. The written word? The printed voices
love their comfortable place, aligned
and cataloged, only defiled by the prying
eye of prurience. Here, limping illiteracy
gets a break — a handicapped parking
place. On my 5pm weekday SRO bus ride,
silent commuters hushed by drudgery look
straight ahead, waiting impatiently for their
stop. In this spent quietude, strange sounds
sometimes penetrate the air: a chicken
clucking, a pig grunting, a cow mooing. I
don't know the guy's name or even what
he looks like — no one ever diverts their
fixed stare, but he's a regular. The barnyard
arias are not continuous, but pop up every
stop or two, perhaps to startle the new
arrivals to our ark on wheels. I smile now,
as I remember him and his lively interjec-
tions into our malaise. I remember few
of the others who hadn't the temerity to

break our burdened silence. Was he a nut? No, the craziness was ours, for not joining in with our own bucolic calls. Maybe, all together singing *Old Mac Donald Had a Farm*, as we tooled down Figueroa Avenue on a 5pm rush-hour hayride. All faces, for this once, with ear to ear, lip-stretching grins. Our shepherd Alex, who drives the flock, is a people person. With five brothers and six sisters, how could he have been anything other? He empathizes with those who ride behind him, and is comforted to a degree, in knowing he supplies at least one of their needs. "Hey Al", he reflects, (he calls himself Al), "there's worse jobs than driving a bus, like no job at all — being the driven and not the driver!" So he goes on, and his riders with him. For 14years he has driven on, through robbery, heart attack, child birth and sporadic gunfire, to keep his appointed rounds. He has gotten us there and back with uncommon (given the variables) regularity. The significant thing is not when he arrives, but that he arrives at all. Here he is now! The doors open, close, and off the tour bus goes, through the heart of dying-to-be urbanity.

Wanda is younger than she looks. Weighted down by burdens and bundles, she has only her man's stained briefs to wear, and his abuse; while every second she bears the packages of family continuity along a pot-holed route. Often she thinks: "Please God, let me sit here a little longer in the unburdened peace of this bus-seat-rocking chair. Don t let that door open yet — not yet." Psssssh! The doors open, close, and off she goes, trudging the seven blocks home to face the never ending constraints of language, poverty and the unsheathed cock. "Someday, I won't get off the bus! I'll just stay on and ride and ride until the bus wears out . Even in the bus graveyard, I'll still be sitting there, in and out of an endless carefree junkyard day-dream. The doors will not open, the doors will not close. And The Father Almighty will see it in his kind heart to call a short recess in The Trail of Wanda."

      Phillip is older than he looks. Families members everywhere, and nothing to give to them, that's why he stays hidden. He sits hunched forward in his seat wondering how long the ride will last, how many times the doors will open and shut before his ride is over. Ducking down, he takes a little hit, just a little one, to get him ten blocks or so — taking life's blocks in manageable multiples of ten. This route has no last stop. The vehicle just turns around and heads back the way it came. His views are through the same window, only of the other side of the street. He swears there's no difference at all between this side and that side, except in the late afternoon when that side's the shady side. At 95°, it's always better to be on the shady side. Phillip has always walked the shady side. Phillip prefers the night, when darkness hides the details. At Pershing Square, the doors open and off he goes to struggle with the minutia of a summer afternoon, and await obscuring night. The doors then close, and Phillip, with all his details, pass out of sight.

Carlos is on the verge of thirteen. For the handsome dark-eyed boy, this is the only way to get to where he's going, for now. He learns bus stop impatience and cynicism along the way. Soon the rites of puberty will portend the rites of membership in a far more exclusive club — The 18th Street Gang. Then, Carlos will never again have to ride LA with strangers. The bus will stop, but Carlos will not get on. Oh Dios! his Mother will cry, get on and ride off to the Getty, the Hollywood Bowl, the Ahmanson Theater, UCLA and beyond. Get on and keep riding mi hijo, to some higher place! Don't make your mother cry Carlos, get on the bus! He hangs on the corner with his home-boys as pssssh! — the bus comes, then goes; the doors open, then close and Carlos remains on the corner, waiting to die with honor, to the funerary drumbeat of a mother's broken heart.

Those on board hold their breath as Alma approaches. The 300 pound octogenarian rocks side to side with a cane in each hand for support. She moves in a pendulum motion, like Stevie Wonder might, playing Chopin's Funeral March. We watch and wonder at her extraordinary tenacity. Now that she's aboard

... there's an audible sigh from her, and us, as she drops into her seat. Vehicles of all kinds accommodate those like Alma, whether with bus-pass or car key, they make their way to grocery store or doctor's office, absolutely refusing to give up their independence, to the dismay of relatives and all those who happen to get in the way. Alma is making her weekly sojourn to the Farmer's Market in Hollywood. Of course, there are markets closer by, but no stars can be seen in them. Things have changed, she thinks, mostly TV actors now, not real stars like there were before. Once Cary Grant's hand touched hers as they both reached for the same cantaloupe. Another time, she's absolutely sure she heard Debbie Reynolds fart. They are real people after all, she remembers thinking. "Is that my stop coming up? What I wouldn't give for a good tomato. Is Jimmy Stewart still alive?" The doors open and close and off she goes, propelled by some miraculous rocking perpetuality.

John sits erect, sure of himself, and his position in life, and on the bus. Dedicated to work, family and conservation, he rides public transport as his ecological duty. He'd readily ride a bicycle, if it weren't a death sentence in LA. He feels the other bus riders know why he's there, and respect his sacrifice. (In fact, the rest of the riders could give a shit. To most, he's just another occupied seat.) He's no threat though, and we all appreciate that. John will keep this up for a couple of months, then tire of the inconvenience, barnyard sounds, and smells. "I tried" he'll tell himself, then pay the ridiculous monthly fee to park his BMW." I do my part in many other ways." he rationalizes, barely hearing those thoughts above his $6000 Bose audio system. We all prefer an empty seat John. These doors will open and close 1000 times, John, and no one will miss you, or remember your noble effort. You may be of some help to humanity John, but you've been no help at all to the riders of Zigzag One.

     Mai Lee is hardly visible — inside seat, back of the bus. She runs a machine in Chinatown, a sewing machine, competing with her brethren from across the sea. Mai Lee works long and hard, but does not sleep long and hard. She dreams of being wrapped in fabric from an endless bolt of cloth, and sewing buttonholes with her hands and feet. She welcomes the mornings, when off she goes to the bus stop. Zigzag #1 deposits her in front of her well oiled machine, where all day she wraps herself in bolts of cloth and sews button holes with her hands and feet, living the same dreams that filled her midnight hours. "Wait!", she often asks herself, "is it day, or is it night?"

The doors open at Center Street. I step
off the merry-go-round, and head for my
refrigerator-carton urban-loft, to transcribe
my thoughts onto the endless ream of dot
matrix printer paper I found in the dumpster
behind Office Depot. I love it here on the
West Bank at sunset, reflecting on my ride
through the heart of the disconnected city
sprawl. At night, I dream that I'm on the
bus again, and at each stop some famous
person climbs aboard. These icons know
my name, and smile at me, and defer to
me. More get on, but none want to get off,
so enamored are they of my company.
So, off we go through the night, a mutual
admiration society of LA bus dreamers. In
silence, we exchange knowing glances, all
of us bound for the same secret place. At
Figueroa and 39th, a dark-skinned, brightly
clad figure races our way. Evelyn Ashford
jumps aboard, still wearing track shoes
and an Olympic gold medal around her
neck. Having just won the 100 meter dash,
the tape did not end her sprint. Snatching
up her golden perdant, she headed
right out the open end of the Coliseum
and onto Zigzag 1, in need of immediate
transport from the hectic scene to feel
sand beneath her winged feet. Evelyn
chose to sit on what little seat was left next
to Alma — her opposite in form and func-
tion. They were a pair sitting there! They
did not speak. Their communication was in
their commingled presence. And all that
cared to look were taken by the contrast:

a short story of glory, juxtaposed with an historical novel of drudgery. Miss Ashford disembarked at the Santa Monica Pier. Stripping down to only her golden medal, she sprinted free across the sandy shore as scores lined the pier to cheer her victory in the naked pursuit of freedom.

One afternoon, at 1st and Grand, Esa Pekka Salonen embarks, fleeing screeching violins and twelve-tonality. He chooses a seat next to Carlos. They rap in accented speech, about contemporary musical forms, each conducting himself with propriety. They each know the score: the musical prodigy, and he who is not likely to get past twenty three. After a short ride of only thirty bars or so, Esa Pekka finds himself longing for stringed instruments and dissonance — Carlos for the harmony of an 18th Street corner. They both would get their wish, as always happens on this particular bus. The doors would close, and off we'd go without them — contrapuntal accents of their recitative lingering in the air.

One gray June day, Rosie O'Donnell climbs aboard, having chosen this mode of transport to avoid the paparazzi on her trip to City Hall, for a marriage license of the homogeneous kind, just now become available. Who, what, or how Rosie fucked — sanctioned or unsanctioned — was of no concern to the other riders, except for Alex our driver, whom she sat directly behind, prating endlessly about things he already knows all about from his devotion to Fox News. Alex was not totally unsympathetic to Rosie's cause: girl fagging he could understand — but guy fagging guy, he could not. At City Hall, the doors open, and out goes Rosie. The doors close and off we go, the echo of her voice, and the images she invoked, still riding along with us in Alex's Right Wing Factored mind.

Out of nowhere appears Edward Scissorhands, sitting at the bus stop, hands flashing in the sun. No sense asking him to fumble for the fare. He carefully navigates the aisle of ducking heads to where Mai Lee sits huddled in her silkworm cocoon. Interesting to see, thought we, what will come of this association. What came of it, is this: With his prowess for cutting fabric, and hers at sewing it, they started their own clothing line, CUT UPS, and conquered the fashion world. All starting here in my dream — she with buttonholing extremities, and he with scissored hands. Now, seamlessly matched, they have abandoned public transportation, and are frequently seen sitting in the back seat of a long black limousine, admiring its upholstery, and giving thanks for their chance encounter on Zigzag1.

In this particular dream, the darkness fades to find: Sitting next to Wanda is Cal Worthington. On Cal's lap, sits his dog Spot. He has come aboard to convert riders to drivers. Moving from seat to seat, he gives his spiel, the same spiel to every rider, exactly: "Nothing to put down! No one tuned down! Go see Cal, Go see Cal, Go see Cal!" After each exclamation, Spot would bark. Entertaining, but futile. A Dodge Charger is not in Wanda's future, nor in the futures of the rest of we bloodless turnips. Undaunted, the dynamic duo disembark near Atlantic Avenue, and head south toward Firestone Boulevard, repeating the chant-bark mantra that helped make LA what it is today. (As every New Yorker knows.)

From somewhere, maybe a West Hollywood gig, Judy Garland boards our bus, and Toto comes with her. (Spot was given that privilege, why not?) Judy does not sit down, but stands in the aisle and sings. Feet planted firmly on our moving stage , arm extended, fingers splayed — she belts and Toto howls. Judy would not stop singing, and Toto would not stop howling. A very emotional experience for all. Finally, our driver had to stop the bus and put them off because no one could stand it anymore. At Pico and Fairfax, the doors opened and off they went, skipping westward down what I'm sure they imagined to be a yellow brick road. And in this dream, it was just that— a Yellow Brick Road leading to Muscle Beach, bordering what was, once upon a time, an Emerald Sea.

With a retinue of twelve, Martha
Stewart comes aboard to commiserate
with John about the sacrifices he has
made, and to make a documentary
about the dangers of riding with the
lowly, and the sensible choice he made
in abandoning his naivety. "Life is least fair
to those who have the most. Those with
nothing, how can they possibly know?"
she explains. "John", Martha continues, "I
fully understand why you prefer a Bavarian
Motor Works headliner to the gray dome
of LA City Lines Bus." Martha has graciously
brought on board servings of crab and
lobster bisque, so that the humble riders
might begin to understand what losing
what they will never have might be like —
had they had it. The incredibly generous
Martha works the ladle herself. From
paper bowls with plastic spoons, weary
fingers attempt to raise the liquid to their
lips — trembling from gratitude and so
many bumps in the road. Unfortunately,
it is impossible to eat soup on a moving
bus, and the bisque ended up here, there,
and in a crack or two. That redolence of
aging crustacean lingered for months, and
served as a reminder to all subsequent
riders that Martha had visited there.
The doors swing open, reverently, at
Temple and Grand.
    From Our Lady of the Angeles
Cathedral, a failed attempt at
Stonehenge, the would-be-Pope, Cardinal
Mahoney, stunning in scarlet (Regaled so,

he is often mistaken for a pimp.) ascends the steps to ride the streets whereon his flock doth graze. As riders with children gather them near, this Holy Shepherd, with crook in hand, hurls truths from the missel, then passes his hat among us. Not just any hat — the inverted mitre is dark and deep. What is dropped in, disappears completely, out of this world and into some unseeable next. Eminently lordly in egress, he steps gracefully off the last step, over the gutter, and onto the sidewalk, where he spreads his royal cape and wings it up into Our Lady's bell tower. There, he beats the bells with his cudgel, and duels the pendulous clappers. The arrhythmic ringing alerts all below that, once again, the batty Crusader has returned to abuse the belfry.

I have dreams other than these — just like those you have. I recognize you! You're the one who sits in the back and softly sings Gospel hymns. Remember me from the night-before-last? I was in the front writing in a little book. I wanted to stand up and sing along with you, but I couldn't make myself do it, not even in our shared dream.

It's late June, overcast, cool, and a bit chilly in the Westinghouse cardboard lofts. The ride around town was as usual: observing grins, sins and a lot of futility. But here, tonight, my candle burns with purpose. From the flickering light, words run down like wax, staining my blank sheet with opaque tears. Can written words give tears more poignancy than they had upon the crier's cheek? Can this be? Words instruct, relate, entertain. Words are not real things. This is not real. Real is not a stop on this bus's route. There are no signs for it — no benches where real waits. Snuffing the candle, I lie back and listen to the cardboard-muffled sound of an LA dry riverbank night. Tomorrow, I will ride again, and pray that on that day, everyone stays on board until Pico meets the shore. The doors fly open, and we all pile out, stack our clothes in a heap, and dance Carmina Burana before Catalina, feeling the freedom of sand and saltwater between our gnarled toes. We stay late ¯o celebrate around the bonfire of our dreaming . Finally, the revelry dissipates, and eyes turn away from each other and into the fire. As the last embers rise, the flicker deserts now anxious eyes. One by one we shake the sand out of our souls and climb back aboard Zigzag1. No one dares look around or speak. The doors that openec, are now shut, and we navigate the fixed course — back to where our ride began. The next morning, in the damp gray dawn, I pull back the pink hibiscus-beach-towel-entry-curtain to analyze the spectrum of the new day's first light. Before me, piddling in a puddle, a carefree sparrow is about to be consumed by feline joy.

...

He Beneath

After the complete emasculation of her
man, Alicia wonders if their relationship can
now be characterized as homosexual. "Is this
an awakening? "Should I tell the Priest? Or,
should I dump him for some authentic pussy?
No, no. Things are just fine as they are."
So they remained. She atop, he beneath.
Often, during their engagements, Phillip
marvels at how much he enjoys getting
fucked in this way.

Part 2:
Early in their relationship Phil realized
that acquiescence was the better course if
the partnership was to last. So, he allowed
the latent lesbian bitch to have her way.

I Want My Daddy!

I want my Daddy! He has promised
me things no Mother could. Elixirs more
powerful than mother's milk, and searing
tears, burning like no woman's would.
And domination. Lessons in cruelty and
intimidation. Life: He will teach me to seed
it, and wrest its essence. Honor: he will
teach me that honor triumphs over love,
and loyalty trumps compassion. And all
about straights and flushes,and how to lie
and politic. All these things he will impart.
Let go of me, my dearest woman-mother!
Let me squirm away to battle. You are
my weakness, he my strength. Hand me
over to him — now! "I no longer wish *To sulk
upon my mother's breast*". Make me your
blood sacrifice. I want my Daddy. I want to
maraud with him, to be the sabre at his side.

I Want My Mommy Back

I want my Mommy back, so I can tell her
how I feel about what she did to me with
her love for me. The fatherless youth she
gave me. So sure was she that loving twice
as much would compensate for the loss of
whiskers and calloused hands; Soft breasts
would cushion the pangs of masculine
identity, and the need to kill wild buffalo on
the great western plains. No guns allowed,
no horses, no rider, no dusty trails. Driven off
the veldt by a white woman's bolt-action
rifle, the noble Indian warrior, emasculated,
retreats to obscurity, his land and honor
lost forever. Copious kisses I could not feel.
Bound by the ambiguity of lust I must, I must
not. Someone tell me how it was for them
so I can know. My mother beat me with a
belt, and dainty buckle welts would rise, but
I could not cry at that humiliation. It was a
weapon that once constrained me in the
womb. I would not cry or moan or speak.
How strange this love of hers, all for me — in
compensation.

Othello

As spring came, Mule longed for the stage
of the Met, and again singing the title role
in Verdi's Othello. A real kick-in–the-ass,
that part. The last time he performed it,
he wowed the audience, receiving a 10
minute standing ovation when he trotted
on stage after the final curtain. Have you
ever seen a Mule cry? There were some
negative comments by the critics about his
stubborn refusal to leave the stage, even
after the audience had left the hall; and
too, his habit of eating the bouquets. But
most dismissed this bizarre behavior as "the
nature of the beast". Some things never
change for tenors. Elmo turned the rap up
to maximum blast, and up from the deep
came Lenore the tube worm, all hot and
bothered, venting her rage on the pair of
hot-rock tuned in lizards sunning themselves
while waiting for an errant bug to violate
their no-fly-zone. She was pacified that this
was an adolescent display, and returned
to foraging in the deep. On her patio chair,
Dame Joan Sutherland assured herself that
this backwater swamp would one day be
oceanfront property. Atlas complained that
if the planet he held got any hotter, he'd
have to drop it, right in the middle of deep

blue Crater Lake, and watch it cool and sink clear out of sight. The Vice President thought this all bullshit, suggesting the only way to save the planet was to destroy it, then let the debris reassemble itself, perhaps in the Andromeda galaxy. The President naively nodded approval of this plan, thinking as he always did, that his VP was only kidding. Ha Ha laughed the President. Ha Ha Ha lastly laughed the VP.

Tiger and the Rose

So then, Tiger climbed up the thorny stem, aiming for the petals of the woman he most admired — who was, at once, responsible for him, the petal, and the thorn. When Tiger reached the rose, the stem could not support the terrible-tiger-weight and bent over nearly touching the ground; whereby Tiger stepped off the stem to a place in the shade of an Acacia tree — where, no longer in pursuit, he wondered what he was doing trying to climb a rose bush in the first place. So it goes in the jungle of our hearts: all manner of things interact and contradict, until the comedy of absurdity is played out, and the actors stand to cheer themselves because there is no audience for their farce. In the alley behind the Opera House, ants run back and forth across the ground, ignorant of Verdi and improbable operatic scenarios. God help us all, if these little spear carriers ever ask themselves why they act the way they do.

Safety Off

Press the button, hear the beep, insert the
key and turn it to the right. Varoooom!
The monster's fire is lit. There you sit, listen
to the throaty roar. Slam it in gear and off
you go, to merge into the arterial flow.
Oh, I love it so. 9mm's at my side. I'll be
pumping off a few rounds when and where
necessary. Maybe an entire clip, maybe
two — depending on the level of frenzy. A
two clip day in LA? It's worse than a jungle
out there. More humans die on the highway
in a day, than all that tigers have killed
from the beginning of tiger-time. I feel an
incident coming on. Safety off. Oh, someone
going to pay dearly for that thoughtless
transgression. Motherfucker cut me off! — a
sin without redemption. This may just be a
two clip day. And who knows who you really
cap? Windows all tinted black. I'll put some
holes in that opacity, so light and fright may
enter in. Who knows what evil transpires
behind those blackened drapes? I am the
projectile of vengeance. No one out here is
without sin. No one dies by accident. I am
your fate, waiting to happen to you. Go
ahead motherfucker, make my morning
commute! To die on the eye10 — how sweet.
You live in your casket fool. Adore and

adorn with tuck and roll, shine the handles, polish the coffin lid. Now ... now, you are prepared to die. Ask forgiveness fool. Pop, pop, pop ....pop! When I go, bury me at the 10/ 405 Interchange — beneath the cloverleaf, turbocharger, weapon, spent cartridges and all. Not too deep! I want to be able to hear the endless roar of tires and the eternally combusting engines of freeway fools taking the Lord's name directly into their brachial vein.

The Next Time

The next time will be different: The round table will be square, The armchair will be a stool, Wednesday will be Monday, Jews will be Muslims, Christians tolerant. Automobiles will be cantaloupe, AIDS — diaper rash, death — elective, today — yesterday, tomorrow — yesterday, and yesterday will stay, forever and completely out of the way. Dreams will be real, and reality a dream. Chemistry will supplant theology, and geography will be a required subject. The next time: I will laugh when I shouldn't, and cry when I shouldn't, and try at all times to be the good boy my Mother and Uncle Albert had hoped for. (My Uncle Albert was a Prince, and lived in a can, but no longer can 'cause California law says "no Princes in cans!") The planet will warm up and dry up and everyone will live in the desert until it dries up too, not an easy thing to do. Then ... the next time there won't be one. Nothing to argue or fight about then. Then, once again, Prince Albert will be united with his Episcopalian can.

The Simple Life

Tumbleweed and manzanita collide at the convergence of desert roads that lead to and away from the simple life, entangling themselves in the most intricate way. Having chosen the desert to avoid complicated involvements, each finds himself bound up with a totally different species. Each was now sure that life as he knew it was over. Then the desert wind that brought them so violently together, rips them apart, each ending up one half of what they had been before. Wounded but separate, they lay in the scorching sun wondering if two so disparate halves could again come together, this time to form a unique hybrid whole.

Part 2:
A broken teacup handle is glued back on — functional yes, chaste no. From it, tea now tastes differently.

The Yellow Car

In a canary yellow 1942 Packard convertible,
I fled with another into the Mojave desert
heat, reluctant to leave an ocean breeze,
and less reluctant to abandon a pregnant
18year old Norwegian blond. My traveling
companions did not last: The escape
vehicle, unable to take the heat, blew her
engine east of Kingman, becoming another
Route 66 roadside casualty of flight. My
equally volatile co-conspirator, undeterred
by our vehicle's demise, raised her pretty
thumb, and continued East without me. No
money for repair, I left the faithless Packard
there, Greyhounding it back to assume the
role of an erstwhile father by the Bay. That
abandoned '42 would someday become
an icon for an era. Idyllic times "before
the war" — the good old days for some,
the same old days for others. Eventual
rescue and restoration did not destroy that
Packard's memory of what it had done
in alliance with the desert sun: turning
an escapee back to face the blushing
cheeks he'd tried to frame in the rear-view
mirror as he headed east in his ill-behaved
convertible. Little did the mother-to-be know
of where I'd been, or what I intended. Years

later we baptized our first child. There were
other children too, and a long, tumultuous,
relationship that somehow lasted. All this
at the behest of a machine that refused to
run, and the reflective power of the Mojave
sun. This is the past. Not the most-part of
the past that doesn't last, but those singular
encounters with failed devices that control
our destiny. Saguaro arms pointed the way,
into, then out of, bitterness and regret.

Three Little Things:

Now written, words glance from side to side
judging their placement on the line.

Singing a different tune, the innovative little
bird is driven from the flock.

She claimed to have read my book, saying
to me: *"How nice it is."* Had she stepped on
my blue swede shoes.

Mary watches television on an average of 5 hours a day. Mary also spends an equal amount of time on the web. What she watches, and the sites she hits, tell us all about Mary. We know more about Mary than Mary knows, or wants to know, about herself. We monitor her every whim. Never ever feel lonely Mary, we are always with you, anticipating your next impulsive act, guiding you to those exact choices we know will fill your wants and needs. Now Mary, be honest, doesn't this make you feel comfortable and secure. Now Mary, tell us, what is it you really want? Just kidding Mary, we already know!

Part 2:
With maxed out credit cards and no buying power, Mary has lost her significance. Sorry Insignificant Mary — Caveat emptor!

Afterword Again

Man needs to believe, it makes him different from all the other stuff. Whether a Paleolithic spear or a Gothic Cathedral, in it ... he places his trust. Growing between man and his beliefs is the infestation of bureaucracy keeping the fingers that launched the spear from touching the bloodied flint. I know I must believe in something, but I don't know what it is. Strip me of everything I know, everyone I love, and all that's in between. Now, let's see if I can figure out what, if anything, separates me from the other stuff. Time to go. Here comes the bus. And, miracle of miracles, it's right on time.

Alone

When I drive I am most alive, Zigging and zagging here and there, I aggravate, gesticulate and shout obscenities that fortunately only I can hear. These encounters are the extent of my socialzing. Any wonder I never seem to have anything civil to say. I prefer to speak in expletives in the friendly confines of my V8 isolation booth.

A Pearl

Maria's spiked heels click on the terrazzo entry floor as she heads toward the front door and a Met production of *La Forza del Destino* . One last look in the console mirror, a subtle adjustment here and there, and all is acceptably arranged. Then in a discreet instant in the history of all things, Maria's Cartier Libre watch band catches on her exquisitely matched natural black pearl necklace. Freed from their tethering they follow each other to the glazed floor, clattering and scattering with an energy openly disdainful of kinetic law. This descent of order into chaos will cause Maria to be late for the opera where she will display the blue veins that black pearls would otherwise have hidden. Later a thorough search on hand and knee finds all but one of the escapees. To find them all is against the law, the one and only *Missing Black Pearl Mystery Law*. The necklace is shorter now. In a dark recess of another dimension, a solitary black jewel wonders, if in his exuberant display of freedom, he propelled himself a tile too far. Occasionally, when clacking toward the front door, Maria will stop at that same console mirror, raise a hand to her throat and reflect on what was missed that day : the overture and first act of a Verdi opera and a single transmutant black pearl.

A Wheat Field

The yard looks like a wheat field, hasn't
been cut in weeks. The boys' job — but shit,
looks like Dad's gotta do it. So on Sunday
morning At 7am (sure to rile the neighbors)
Dad digs through the garage and rolls out
the old power mower, the one the boys'
complained doesn't work and how they'd
be more than glac to cut the lawn If he
would just by a new one, Checks for fuel
and begins pulling, and continues yanking
on the old girl for the longest time. Finally
with great smoke cnd sputter she comes
to life. Dad hasn't cut a blade yet, but
already he is red-faced and sweating. Two
rows in, she chocks, gasps and quits. Dad
yanks, sweats, mumbles and gets redder
and redder. Finally the starter rope brakes
off in his hand. "Worthless fucking kids!" he
yells aloud. Dad then grabs the handle with
both hands and Begins spinning old Lady
Kenmore like he was a hammer thrower and
she the hammer. When Dad lets go of the
machine, something lets go in dad's back
too, and both man and machine lie equally
disabled in the tall grass. This was the end of
the old Kenmore rotary And the beginning
of the end for Dad too. His back was fucked
up good, he couldn't work anymore and
had to go on disability. Handfuls of Vicodin
mitigate the back pain but nothing could
relieve the pain he suffers from living with
a houseful of useless morons. Dad soon

added alcohol to his prescriptions list. Dad was in rapid retreat. Before long, he had retreated into debilitating and rancorous despair. Through it all, the dysfunctional Lady lay where she was heaved on that fateful day, just about invisible in the overgrowth. Mom and the boys could take the abuse no more, they moved out leaving dad to face an incompetent world alone. Dad become a recluse, seldom seen by the neighbors who thought it just as well. Pizza, booze, meds delivered to the door, Payment propped in the letter slot. The city came out and mowed down what was considered a blight on the community, except for a swath around the miscreant mower. A sick joke thought he, likely the work of his mindless wife. They mailed him the bill. As Winter neared It became clear to Dad that he wouldn't be around for the holidays. On a Friday afternoon in late October Just past four in the afternoon, Dad straightened up a few things around the house, to satisfy himself that he still had a sense of humor, then drew a bath in the multi-ringed upstairs tub. Getting in the tub was a real struggle, but he did it. He drew water as hot as he could stand, took a handful of pink pills, A long hit form a plastic half-gallon bottle of tequila, then with a newly bladed Exacto knife, he sliced calmly and deeply into each wrist. As the hot water reddened, Dad whitened. He looked up through the steam at the beads of moisture forming on the ceiling, thinking with a twisted grin, "Here's one mess I'm not going to have to clean up". His last thoughts before drifting into oblivion were not of family, or regret, but of a lone stretch of highway he remembers from long ago where stood a line of beautiful pink hollyhocks, some reaching maybe ten feet tall. That was all. The family buried Paul with uncharacteristic respect. Paul Junior, his oldest son gave the eulogy: "No one ever really understood my dad. Somewhere way deep down, the man was a saint." The old bastard was laid to rest in a lovely part of Father of Grace Cemetery. As long as I can remember, his sons visited his grave weekly, making sure there were fresh flowers there in all seasons, and the grass above their dead Dad's head was always weed-free and neatly trimmed.

***

Baa, Baa

Baa, baa went the lamb chop.
Oink, oink went the pork chop.
Chop, slice went the butcher.
Sizzle, sizzle went the griddle.
Chomp, chomp went the carnivore.
Need I trace more of what follows
on this pathway to the gallows?

Beach Combers

We took a long walk on the beach — my
better half and I. A beautiful mid-September
day. We spoke of nothing important. Looking
back, it was this vanilla prattle that made
the trek so enjoyable. The absolute delight
in being able to converse for so long a time
without grievance or demand. Later, we
lunched at the beach, and although others
joined us, meaningless chit-chat pervaded,
while invective and petty annoyance
remained anchored far out in the cove. In
that way, the afternoon past; and a gentle
breeze came ashore to accompany our
azure discourse.

Crystal Cove, September 2009

Consolation

Mornings like this one are coming more frequently. The gang has cleared, the songs of the 80's tease memories from my soul, and I feel with numbing remorse, what tightly surrounds me here and now, is all there is and all there will be — ever. This feeling of hopelessness seeps through the real-wood designer blinds and illuminates my slumping figure at the tombstone-cold, polished granite kitchen countertop. All the appliances are stainless steel — I am not. I suppose these feelings of futility are shared by many other women, and likely diagnosed by their husbands and Good Housekeeping as hormonal imbalance. No consolation. My coffee's cold; and, God help me, I just smoked my first cigarette in four years. I enable lives, but have none of my own. I am dependent on enabling. Is that not noble? Should I not be satisfied to sacrifice my life so that those I love will find fulfillment in their own? *Karli, dear Karli, it makes no sense to dress in sackcloth, you'll only have to change, you have a Yoga class at Ten. It's The Schedule that will save you my dear, it's all about staying on The Schedule.* Lunch with Barb and Anna. I'll have the dinner salad, rye crisp and iced tea. We'll chatter endlessly about how family annoyances, taken collectively, are what happiness is all about; how childlike all men are, and the probability of orgasm in prepubescent girls.

We share a couple of hours rationalizing our non-lives into the fulfilling adventures of the modern woman. Shit, that's my cell phone singing "*Every Breath You Take*". *Hello*. [blah, blah, blah] It's the school, Eric's been sneezing and spraying snot and disease all over the classroom. I've got to go get him. Well, there goes The Schedule. Hi sweetheart. *Hi Mom*. Feeling poorly, are you my dear? *Yes Mom, I think I gotta bug.* Right on schedule! I respond, realizing that ... somewhere, I must have penciled this in.

***

Dick and Jane

Dick and Jane played together from an very early age. The games they played were innocent exploratory fun. (Not always socially acceptable, but harmless.) As they matured, the games became more and more intense, and "fun" could no longer adequately describe them. This playfulness would finally reach the level of ecstatic pain. Almost immediately after the wedding the intensity of their fun began to wane. Just before the divorce, the games they played were all pain and no ecstasy. Maybe if Dick and Jane hadn't fooled around so much at an early age, their marriage would have lasted longer; although this would likely have only delayed the inevitable. Now, Dick and Jane go their separate ways, each seeking to recapture the intensity of those early years before their trip down the aisle of matrimony. Thereafter, they did a lot of sexual experimentation, doing some really weird shit, in an attempt to recapture those illusive early raptures. But, the thrill was gone, and so were those exotic places only innocent fumbling can discover.

Erector Set

For Christmas my wife bought me an Erector Set, thinking she had purchased an Erection Set!

Roped

The marriage broke up after only six months. Incompatibility was the issue. She wanted to be tied down, and so did he.

Eva

Evangeline, drinks her Gallo wine at the corner of Hollywood &Vine, financing her preference for juiced up muscatel by offering discounts: hundred dollar blowjobs at ten bucks a pop. Muskat was the only thing that could sufficiently dilute the lingering essence of semen and cock-cheese from her palette. Evangeline can be seen most nights beneath the crossed signs that mark the four corners of Hollywood & Vine. Eva's saving for a condo in Palm Springs. She's got eleven hundred so far.
A car loaded with loaded kids passes screaming: *Suck this, bitch!* Eva just smiles. If they only knew how faithless youth can be.

Fleas

Fleas have the circus,
Mice — the treadmill.
Cockroaches have the hotel,
Benches — the bus stop.
Beer drinkers have the saloon,
Hairdressers — the salon.
Soldiers have Arlington,
Politicians — each other.
The Populace — WalMart.

It seemed to him

JFK Jr. took a flight into the gloaming. He invited others — for surely he of all people was qualified to navigate fate's beckon. The world turned upside down, it seemed to him, so up he went, and found the Sea. Oceanus was annoyed by this senseless intrusion. Equally annoyed were we.

Janet

At forty-four, Janet finally had her teeth fixed. When Harold, her husband, saw his wife's new smile, all he could think of was a blow-job. Same woman, from neck down, from neck up, she was all head. At first, Janet was delighted with her husband's intense new interest in her. But she soon realized his new passion was limited to her renovated mouth. *Great for him*, she thought, *but what about me?* Six months in, she just couldn't swallow it anymore, and returned to the reciprocation of her dildo; while her hubby reactivated his web porno sights, and returned to the comfort of his supplicating fist. Janet and Harold now climax in separate rooms. One overhearing their nocturnal cries of passion, would assume intimacy, and they'd be right — the bad and the beautiful visit each, individually, almost every night.

Laying Waste

It's late August and the blacktop is hot, as
hot as it will ever be. School doors open
again, opening wider than they've ever
been, to accommodate students who
are wider than they've ever been. Who's
ample forms, upon matriculation, support
minds that are narrower than they've ever
been. These shrink-wrapped psyches focus
laser-like on the single goal they have
been prepared for from the first time their
highchairs was turned toward the flat screen.
It's consumption that makes their world go
round. And when everybody has all there
is and there's nothing more to want? What
then? Heaven on earth? Hardly. Today's
chic is engineered into obsolescence,
and the must-haves become the quaint
collectables of another era (last year).
Thereby, free-market economies sustain
themselves by perpetuating the must have
syndrome to which it owes its life. It's the
middle of December now, and the black-
top is as cold as it will ever be as foot-prints
and tire tracks race to fill the stockings and
max out plastic. There's great joy in the utility
of this: Instead of buying a gift likely returned,
I use my piece of plastic to buy someone
else a piece of plastic — a Gift Card. Now
the recipient doesn't redeem it, but keeps
the card and uses it as a birthday gift for
someone else. Then, this someone saves that
Birthday plastic, and I get it back the next

Christmas — as my gift. What goes around, comes around, The cycle is 365 days.   It's June now, and the school doors stretch wide to allow egress to the bar-coded students who have achieved maximum girth, and are ready to hit the beach, provided they possess the proper accoutrements, including but not limited to: a this year's bathing suit, swim fins, wetsuit, boogy-board, currently acceptable beach towel, beach chair, umbrella, matt, sun screen, sunglasses, cell phone, and a ride on anything except a municipal bus.

***

Love You

Bill and Mary are halfway through dinner in total silence. Finally:
Mary: I hate my job!
Bill: I hate my job!
Mary: I hate my job more than you hate your job!
Bill: Impossible! I hate it when you say that.
Mary: I share that feeling with you.
Bill: Then, that's about all we share. *Adding, sotto voce:* Bitch.
Mary: And whose fault is that, bitch!
Bill: Sweet little Mary, I hate your fucking ass!
Mary: How about this: I hate your fucking!
Bill: Listen Mary, let's please stop this before it becomes serious and we say things we'll regret later.
Mary: Yes, yes Bill, you're right. Let's stop this now. Please forgive me.
Bill: You're forgiven. God, I love you!
Mary: Not nearly as much as I love you!

Mary Anne

Mary Anne died yesterday at 4:14pm, on the 12th of March, 2001, 23 days into here 84th year, at 5127 North Tower Avenue, in room 422, in bed A. She was partially warped in a backless gown, supported beneath by a rubber sheet, and covered by a threadbare cotton blanket. Mary Anne has just now completed her slow determined crossing from comatose to the shores of oblivion. As she crossed, she reached down into the river with arthritic fingers and was surprised at how comfortably warm the water was. Mary Anne then moistened her hair and brow. "Finally!" she murmured, and could murmur no more, having just then made contact with the other shore.

Negative Particularity

John sat staring at ... nothing in particular.
Thinking of ... nothing in particular. The day
was unusually gray and his eyes reflected
that. John was not waiting for the fog to
clear; he preferred to remain transfixed:
to see ... nothing in particular, to feel ...
nothing in particular. John often wondered if
he might be dead.
"Would you care for anything else?"
interrupted the waitress's voice.
"Yes" John mumbled, *and hesitated.*
"Anything in particular?" she asked.
"Yes", responded John, *"nothing in
particular."*
The obliging waitress promptly delivered that
which was ordered, and John consumed
same in the blink of an eye. Usually a
generous tipper, on this occasion, John
had no advise for the server. The waitress
understood. She herself was familiar with the
syndrome of Negative Particularity.

Cynthia has destroyed more happy homes
than a Category Five Hurricane. Cynthia's
a temptress, the femme fatale of every
avenue and alleyway in central LA. She's a
Medusa whose look turns pendulous heads
into a phalli of stone. The village men are
helpless to resist investigating the mysteries
of her dank bower. Like ferrous coins, they
are drawn to her magnetic slot. After
draining them of their shekels, she reverses
the field. What's up — now's down. Every
month or two, when I've saved sufficient
coin, I spend an hour in the whirling ecstasy
of a Cynthian tarantella. Her full lips and
port wine sweetened breath devastate
social order. A single taste of her turns all
of life's other servings into oatmeal and
margarine-slathered white bread. *When will
we dance again dear Cynthia? Maybe in
January, when all is cold and gray, you will
again incinerate my day with the aroma
of windblown fresh cut cannabis and wild
mushrooms picked from the shadow of your
hem.* January's here, and all the gifts I didn't
want are going back. I go about, rubbing
shoulders with those returning the useless
gifts I gave. Superficial senseless shit, this
trading of useless things. Now that the
Indian-giving's done, and the stress of
the holidays awaits the exacerbation of
incoming bills, I long for the soothing balm
of Cynthia's touch and smell. It's time we
meet again, to release the bane of forced

reciprocation by sucking each other dry of
Yuletide resolutions. Grand, Olive, 5th Street,
Pershing Square — can't find her anywhere.
Armando, the friendly bartender, swears
he'd seen her the night before, curled up,
not with, but in a bottle of tequila. She,
thought he, had transmuted into a pickled
she-worm. I order a double shot: lick the
salt, suck the lime, then repeat the ritual
thrice more. ... *Fuck it!* ... *I'm ready* . *Let me
see that bottle wherein my Cynthia resides.*
Armando went right to it, grasp it by the
neck, and placed it before me. I stare in,
focus then refocus. There is something about
the eyes, something about those eyes.
Que pasa Senora Gusano? I venture. No
response. *Give me another double*, I order,
and this time put her in it! Without gagging,
I drink the drink and gulp the worm. There's
great satisfaction in knowing no one else will
ever have her — if that was her. Staggering
and stumbling, my bunk saves me from
the floor. I dream of butterflies, larvae and
grotesque dragons eating Tabasco-sauced
young virgins, feet first. Consciousness comes
late the next morning. Squinting through a
dense haze, my nose leads my eyes to a
puddle of puke spread below me — a gift
delivered to the night. Amid the sour slime
lies this wiggling thing. There is something
about the eyes. Through my garret window,
gray beams illuminate the morning-after,
and two night-crawlers on the ledge of
Dante's Second Circle, look down into
another day in the tar-pit of LA.

Nothing to eat

Off to the grocery store to amble through
aisles of polished apples, few of them red
or really red. Crew-cut carrots, flourishing
radishes, lettuce bergs, layered zucchini
and green bananas ripped unripe from the
stalk. I take one of these, three of those,
encounter scallions of interest and ring the
yellow, green, and red of bell peppers. Just
across the isle looking out over the gondolas
of polished color, the mayonnaise and
Campbell's soup rub labels with Kosher
pickles and Greek olives. Then I enter pasta
lane where sanity holds sway. I won't go
on — you know all about the stores of piled
up, stacked up lined up eatable things
being conveyed, scanned and bagged,
then carted to the kitchen where inevitalbly
is heard these discouraging words: "How
come there's never anything to eat around
here?"

On Criticism

There is no criticism harsher than silence, no repartee more revealing than that stifled by politeness, no ridicule more hurtful than that implied.

Once

Love in the eyes is unmistakable — cannot
be feigned. Its vision lasts forever, well after
the flame flickers away. You'll never forget
that wordless spell — cast, caught, fumbled
and broken by time's errant play. Futility
follows the search to recapture those totally
surrendered eyes.

Rules

Who makes these rules? A play needs
neither words nor a venue. Art is blustery
and formless, like the invisible movement
of the air. Music too is soundless, save the
beating or our hearts. Poetry is, or should be,
lawless. Write poetry to avoid the rules. Form
puzzles and complicates. Why this need to
circumscribe. We do nature no justice by
reducing her essence to a grain of sand. On
every level nature seeks instability — to break
its bounds, to fly into chaos. We have two
choices, always two choices. Who makes
these rules?

Moss covers the trees, and crocks line up endlessly to feed on habits dying slowly in the hot humid air, gobbling black and white regurgitating gray while the old way drapes the cypress. "I'm here to say!" echoes in the bayou night and steaming day. The river runs through it all, and ferries up and down it all. Barges of coal pay and take their toll. There'll be Mississippi in Pittsburgh till the end of time, as in the hills of Kentucky asbestos decorates the southern pine. The folk decorate themselves with leaded paint and eat their pone with rotting teeth, hold up their pajamas with suspenders, and call a spade a spade. All's as American as the banana, or the *Ring Cycle* in Alabama.

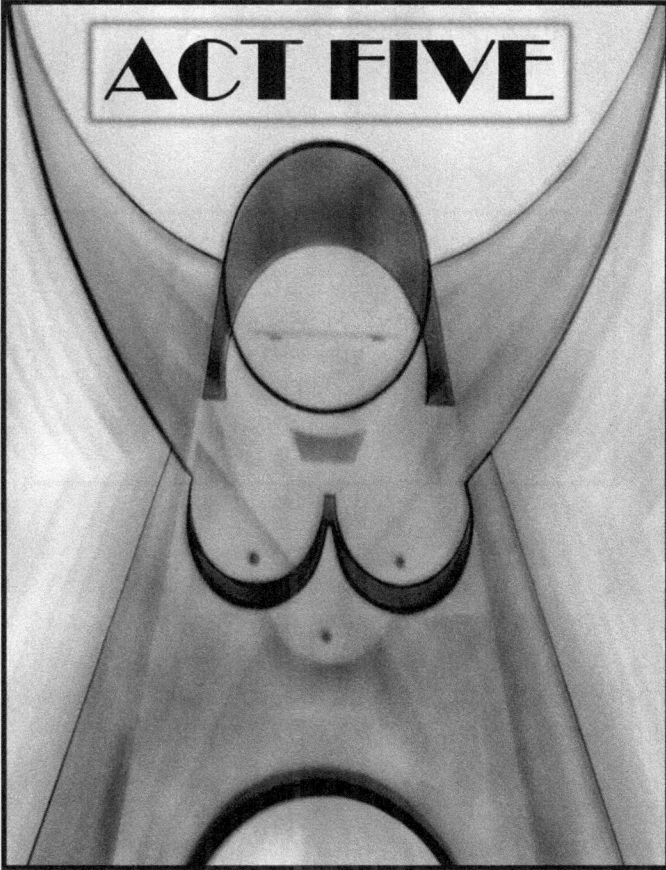

The playbill says ACT 5 and I'm wondering if this is a one act play or have four other acts preceded it? Is the play so long that each act requires its own performance? Oh God, not another Ring Cycle. We'll see. A sign at the box office reads:

ACT 5 — PREMIER PERFORMANCE
A PLAY IN FIVE SCENES BY
WF POSTLE
ALL SEATS $25
LIMITED SEATING (125)
A CAST OF HUNDREDS!

Considering the confines of the venue and the size of the cast, this may be a production worth seeing from a logistical point of view, at least until the Fire Marshal arrives. Two tickets to the play please. You've sold out? Wow. What about future performances? What do you mean there won't be any? "Act Five is the last act. The last act is just that, the last act, nothing follows the last act." That makes no sense in any number of ways. "Making sense is irrelevant. I shouldn't be telling you this but, there are no seats available because the cast is so large there just isn't room enough for an audience."

Now that is way beyond nonsensical, it's absurd! "I agree with you." So, if there are no tickets to be sold, what are you doing in the ticket booth? "I must ask you to move along sir, there are others waiting to not get in."

The houselights dim and the play is about to begin with actors acting as they seldom do, being actors and the audience too.

ACT 5, SCENE ONE:

AUTHOR: Two figures sit on a flattened Maytag washing machine carton, their backs propped up against the front of Stein's Jewelry Store. It had been a balmy night so Joe and Louie slept well. Already Broadway Boulevard's near dead are coming back to near-life.

JOE: Hello, I'm Joe, and this is my dog Louie. You don't know us, but you soon will. That is, what we choose to reveal to you. Here's a short, myopic bio: I was born an anarchist, became obsessed with masturbation before I could talk, and when I started to talk I had a stutter which I was told was the result of — you guessed it. I embraced Judaism just in time to suffer through a painful bar mitzvah. Painful because of the circumcision that immediately preceded it. Soon after, I ran away, hitchhiked actually, to San Francisco where I was delighted to discovered that Judaism and homosexuality were compatible. Then, I entered my dark period: becoming simultaneously a vegan and a closet Republican (Very dark and very crowded in there.). Concurrently, I practiced self-defilement long before tattooing became fashionable, fucked everything of any gender that walked, and some things that didn't, through every orifice real or imagined. All these adventures and many more I had before the age of twenty-four. What's happened since, well, you don't really want to know. I'm here, now, that's all that should matter. Let's skip all the intervening clutter and jump right to that pivotal moment when I was bolted awake by the realization that everything was gone. That is was the last day I'd have a place to stay, nothing in my pockets, broke. Everything of value hocked, all bridges and friends burned, broke. The suicide watch was on, and I was the only one watching. I wasn't worried though, coward that I am, I'd be the last one to walk out on this play before the denouement had even begun. Let's move on to the present.

We, Louie and me, are still broke with no place to go. Did I already mention that? Anyway, we have absolutely nothing except each other. But, I guess, you can't have less than nothing, right? That's the optimist in me talking. No one thing's to blame for our situation except me, I accept that. No genetic component, wasn't dealt a bad hand, wasn't beaten by my father or molested by the Rabbi, none of those things. It is what it is because I am who I am. No bitterness in me. And why should there be? I knew what I was doing when I did what I did. It's not like I didn't know what the consequences of my actions would be — I did. Hell, I made informed choices. Hey, I spent a year and a half at Berkeley. The information may have been suspect, but who gives a shit about details. Not me. That's just who I am and why I do what I do and why I'm where I am. We're diamonds en plein air Louie, just we're not in the window, but just-outside-just-below-the-window diamonds — diamonds in the rough. Sidewalk diamonds. We call the sidewalk home. Louie and I are closer to its unyielding yet indiscriminate surface than to any other man-made object. This concrete slab supports our moans and groans and dreams of marble floors, twelve-foot paneled doors and chicken-liver pâté. When we die, let our ashes be added to the mixer that pours a pathway, a walkway, the promenade. Then we will, for a very long time, support those of every kind that come and go. A firm bed for the weary, a canvas for the chalked hand, a venue for hop-scotch with we two interred in support of it all. A horizontal wall for all those who use our surface without an inkling of what we have laid down for them. I take Louie's passivity as concurrence.

LOUIE: Blah, blah, blah. There's no short answers with this guy, Don't get me wrong, I love him to death, but Joe, come on, give it a rest.

[The jewelry store owner appears.]

MR. STEIN: Good morning fellas, time to move on. Be sure to take everything with you — you know the drill.

JOE: Louie, stop begging!

AUTHOR: Mr. Stein pulls a gingersnap from his pocket, snaps the ginger snap in half and gives a piece to an erect Louie and half to himself. Louie loves Mr. Stein' pocket but wonders about his manners 'cause Joe never gets offered any. Maybe, thought Louie, it's because half a whole consists of only two pieces.

AUTHOR: Now the two were off to the second stop on their Stations of the Broken Cross: the Walk With Jesus Mission for a cup of coffee, two donuts and a prayer. Joe has been saved many times. Joe never tires of being saved. It's simple mathematics, one of these times it's bound to stick. And in the meantime, the coffee is almost always hot, and the donuts no more than a day old.

LOUIE: Donuts good! Salvation good too! Cats have only nine lives, so what's not to like about forever?

AUTHOR: Penance paid and breakfast downed, the two march to the next station: The City Park, where they will sit and prioritize all that passes before them.

[The author, in an effort to lengthen the per-formance of his one act play has added entertaining diversions between each scene. He believes this the first time the "divertimento" have been used in this way.

[Divertimento: A one-armed juggler performs the extraordinary feat of juggling two running chain saws and a fully lit Menorah while singing Das Deutschlandlied.]

SCENE TWO:

[On a park bench.]

JOE: We sit on this bench every morning, rain or shine, watching what the day sends by. I like the dogs best — Louie too, then the birds and then the squirrels, then the little kids. Adult people, not so much. What they garb themselves in is another matter. I like the bright oranges and baby blues, tams, bonnets, baseball caps, tank tops, flip flops. I study the faces, the beaks, the tails too, ever cautious not make eye contact. We have nothing to say to them, we just want to observe, to compare them to us, to give each a relative value.

LOUIE: The fact is I have absolutely no input on these matters, nor do I care to pass judgement on anything or anyone. Call me canine copacetic.

[An elderly fellow supported by a cane takes a seat on the other end of the bench.]

OLD DUDE: Good morning to you both.

JOE: Absolutely

OLD DUDE: Nice day.

JOE: Absolutely.

JOE: Go ahead, you're welcome to sit down — with this caveat: Please don't try to start a conversation. By the way, I'm Joe, he's Louie. We sit here every day – weather permitting. We observe. We two are the Great Observers. And everything we observe we evaluate and place in order. That butterfly, see it there, would have a place well ahead of that man wearing the starched collar. The cocker spaniel over there has a place well ahead of the hand that's holding his leash. We are creating The True Order of All Things. And you good fellow, although we have exchanged but a word or two, I would give you a preliminary placement somewhere between the Afghan my grandmother knitted for my sickly brother (who fully recovered), and the rusty backyard swing I fell off of and broke my left arm when I was ten. You needn't respond, I prefer that you didn't. Words, more often than not, necessitate the reordering of things. We hate to rearrange.

OLD DUDE: That's very generous of you. Your invitation to join you, and no verbal intercourse fits my style perfectly.

JOE: What exactly do you mean by "your style" and "verbal intercourse".

OLD DUDE: Now you see, you've already broken your rule about engaging in conversation.

JOE: Right! You're right, I won't say

another word. But, I've got to know what you mean by "verbal intercourse". That doesn't have anything to do with... like... a blowjob does it? If it does, you're barking up the wrong tree old dude, Louie and me are laser straight.

OLD DUDE: What I refer to is the conversation we are having right now. I'd say you could be just slightly homophobic.

JOE: Sorry, I'll keep my mouth, excuse me, orifice shut.

OLD DUDE: I will reciprocate. And by the way, you have beautiful lips.

JOE: What the fuck!

OLD DUDE: Yes, homophobic.

Louie: Hey, I kind of like this guy. This is why we have no friends.

AUTHOR: The Old Dude soon leaves, bored with the ensuing silence. After an hour or so of assigning people, places and things to the Great Order, the two were off to Station Four: The Greyhound Bus Terminal, where Joe would perform the miracle of bathing fully clothed without getting his clothing wet, leaving Louie tied to the news stand out front. The locals knew and liked Louie, and if they didn't, Louie had demonstrated in the past that he could take care of himself.

[Divertimento: Recital of the John Henry Titus poem The Face Upon the Barroom Floor by local members of the WCTU.]

SCENE THREE:

AUTHOR: In the worn down Greyhound Bus Station, that deserved recognition as an historical monument as much as any other building in the town, a handsome, conservatively dressed middle-aged man is sitting on a bench reading a book bearing the title: Atlas Shrugged. This man bears a striking resemblance to the Republican candidate for the presidency of the United States. Our Joe enters the terminal and catches sight of Mr. Jones. Joe walks back and forth a few times studying the man with the book and a familiar look.

JOE [to himself]: No, it can't be. Alone in a bus station in this town? No way!

AUTHOR: Joe's just got to investigate the possibility of the impossible, and takes a seat on the bench next to, but not too close to, Mr. Jones.]

JOE: Excuse me sir, but do you know how much you look like that Republican guy who's wants to be president?

MR. JONES: Yes, I get that all the time.

JOE: I know this may sound stupid, but, are you that guy?

MR. JONES: I'm sorry to disappoint you, but no, I'm not that guy. As a matter of fact, I find contemporary politics and politicians generally offensive.

JOE: Oh I'm not disappointed at all. It's really kind of cool you looking so much like him and the way you feel about politics. I feel kind of the same way you do, and what's more of a coincidence, people used to say I looked a lot like JFK.

MR. JONES: That's nothing to be proud of.

JOE: Excuse me, say again.

AUTHOR: A long silence ensues and Joe gets up, makes a couple of circuits of the station, then after some hesitation, sits back down.

JOE: You were saying something about Jack Kennedy?

MR. JONES: I'd rather not go into it, It's past history.

JOE: History written by whom?

MR. JONES: The true history, Christian moral history. The divine take on those who have guided and misguided this country of ours. The way to our salvation is through generosity: generosity of spirit allowing a generosity of wealth. We are bound by the tethers of government. To be free, really free, we most loosen those constraints that bind us, that inhibits our ... generosity.

JOE: That sounds like a political speech or a sermon to me. Are you through?

MR. JONES: Oh no, I've hardly begun. The real American dream has been corrupted by ...

JOE: Hold on a minute! Can I say something?

MR. JONES: By all means Joe, speak. That's what I'm here for, to hear what Joe has to say.

JOE: Are you sure you're not running for something. You're sounding just like a preacher or a politician, or worse: a preacher/politician.

MR. JONES: No Joe, I'm just trying to connect with the average American male, to get a feel for him. You are the average American male, right Joe? You are a guy Joe, in the anatomical sense, right? These days one never knows who's what.

JOE: That's affirmative. Except for not having a job, a car or a place to live, I consider myself pretty much the average straight American male. Look at me, could I be anything else?

MR. JONES: Joe, I'll take your word for it. I could tell right off there was something fiftieth percentile about you. Joe, I think we could be friends. Yes, I'm sure of it, we could be friends, at least through the first part of November. What do you say, friends?

JOE: : I'll tell ya Mr. Jones, you're a nice looking dude, dress sharp, smell good, seem smart enough, book under your arm and all, but there's something about you I feel hard to relate to. As you said, I'm just your average dude, sort of, just using the bus station head. What I'm trying to say is this: I look like I belong in here, you don't. Go into that pisser, look around, I'll bet if you hung out all day in there you wouldn't see another straight guy who looks or thinks like you. You look more like a prop the Greyhound people put in here to give the place some class; to try and deceive potential travelers into thinking that you're the kind of guy who rides the Greyhound bus. You and I both know that's bull shit. Would you get on one of those lice-mobiles?

MR. JONES: Yes, I'd ride one of those buses, but I'd have to be the driver. Joe, I'm real. I'm just trying to find out what you people do and think.

JOE: Funny. What's this "you people shit"? Best I leave now before this encounter turns physical.

MR. JONES: I'm very sorry to see you go Joe. I didn't mean to be offensive. What I have to offer is your and this country's salvation. Joe, do you believe in God?

JOE: Who's God?

MR. JONES: Joe, there is only one God.

JOE: Well, now that you've brought the subject up, I have a problem with that. There's a desperate need for more Gods. One God fits all doesn't work anymore. Never worked very well in the first place and even more so in the twenty-first century. It's logistics: a single deity is inadequate to serve billions of individual s needs. A Pantheon appeals to me. Divide and provide. Now take for example fertility rites? What, for instance, can a bachelor born of a virgin possibly know about the joys of the reproductive process. Better the purview of a pregnant female. Let's divide up the jobs — specialize, privatize. Like in olden times, no more one size fits all. An unfaithful husband? Girl, have we got the God for you.

MR JONES: We've been there, done that. Didn't work then, won't work now. Trust me on this one.

JOE: Are you sure you're who you say you are?

MR. JONES: Joe, I know exactly who I am, and who I am would like to count you as a friend, at least for a little while.

JOE: What the fuck, why not. It'll be my good deed for the day.

MR. JONES: Can we shake on that?

JOE: Sure, why not. Here, give me five.

AUTHOR: With the handshake, a $5 dollar bill is transferred from Mr. Jones's hand to Joe's. Nothing else was said, and Joe headed for the restroom not quite sure if Mr. Jones understood what he meant by his offer to shake hands, but damned glad to have the fiver. Washing up, Joe looked at himself in the distorting metal mirror and wondered if the encounter he just had really happened. Looking down at the picture of Abe Lincoln he held in his hand, Joe was reasonably assured that it did. Meanwhile, Mr. Jones examines the bus schedule he is using to book mark Atlas Shrugged. The bus for Allentown departs at 2pm, leaving plenty of time for another encounter or two with the average Joe. And maybe, he could finish rereading Part 1, Chapter 9, Section 2 of his prayer book.

LOUIE: And where have I been during this lengthy encounter? Tethered to a newspaper vending machine that offers up pornography. You might be surprised at who buys this stuff. The indignity of it all.

[Divertimento: Counter-tenor Joe Joe Moore, in black-face, sings Gershwin's Old Man River.]

SCENE FOUR:

AUTHOR: After leaving the station Joe and Louie headed back to the park for some lunch followed by a session of supine transcendental meditation. They stop at the market and buy a loaf of white bread, a package of baloney, a 2 liter bottle of Pepsi and a Super Lotto quick-pick — thanks to the generosity of Mr. Jones, and they have a picnic in the park.

JOE: Damn that was good eatin'!

AUTHOR: Burping in unison with his master, Louie again concurs. With his hands clasped behind his head and Louie's head resting on this thigh, Joe reflects on Mr. Jones and where he belonged in The True Order of All Things. He finally concluded that the appropriate spot was somewhere between Adam Smith and Joseph Smith. And this day, where would he place this day in the true order of all days? Joe decided to just turn off the grader, and enjoy the moment. Feeling the coolness of the grass on his back and the warmness of Louie's head on his thigh, Joe felt that this particular view of the world on this particular day was special.

JOE: You know Louie, it just doesn't get any better than this.

AUTHOR: Louie would certainly concur, had he been awake.

LOUIE: Louie is awake — just resting my eyes. But I've got to agree, or concur if you like, with him on this one. Now if you'll excuse me, I will again assume my default position.

[Divertimento: Ninety year old Faye de Long tap dances to Rimsky-Korsakov's The Flight of the Bumble Bee, then promptly expires. (It's an act, for God's sake!)]

SCENE FIVE:

AUTHOR: The Sunset Tavern has this great cocktail hour. Cheapest drinks in town unless you drink at home, if you have a home. But you know what they say: "A real home is where you can get shit-faced without interference". Joe's not a regular, he's had his bouts with overconsumption, but libation is really not his thing, though he does stop by occasionally when he feels the need for some mano-a-mano conversation, and can round up a few bucks. This afternoon is one of those times. Louie is tethered to newspaper rack, reluctantly exposing himself to secondary smoke inhalation, but with plenty of company, seeing how, to Joe's great amazement, smoking's is now banned in bars, and the patrons actually put up with that shit. Barney the bartender's been around a long time and knows Joe as well as anyone. Barney likes Joe about half the time, that being the first half of Joe's visits. The feeling is mutual half the time,

LOUIE: Here I am again on the outside looking in. Being tied to a rack that dispenses the New York Times does not guarantee contact with a better class of citizen.As a matter of fact, some of those who carry The Times rolled up under their arm have a copy of Teen Pussy, in their waistband. You just never know do you?

JOE: Before we go in, let me just say this: For sure, some think of us as a ne'er-do-well laggards for sure, but we like to think of ourselves as unencumbered free spirits. Looking around in this dungeon called the Sunset Saloon I see a bunch of losers — and most of them don't even know it. And the worst kind of losers are those that think they're winners. The self-professed failure I can tolerate. The self-diluted I cannot. We fit into neither category. Louie and I have placed ourselves in a group apart. We comprise a unique cabal whose members have neither obligation or regret. So rare are we, so few, so exclusive. Let's see if we can sponge a libation or two.

JOE: Hey everybody, I'm here. Please, please, don't get up.

AUTHOR: Joe takes a seat at the end of the bar where he is like likely to find Barney most of the time.

JOE: Afternoon Barn.

BARNEY: Hey Joe. Get any lately?

JOE: Any what?

BARNEY: Pussy.

JOE: Sorry, I have a dog.

BARNEY: You know what I mean.

JOE: No I don't.

BARNEY: Joe, you're a hard guy to talk to.

JOE: You're a hard guy to talk with.

BARNEY: How about this weather?

JOE: How about it. A real controversial subject.

BARNEY: Joe, you want to be left alone?

JOE: No ... no. Sorry, it just that it's the first of the month. All the bills are due and I'm busted.

BARNEY: What bills? You're homeless man, you aint got no fucking bills!

JOE: What's that got to do with it? It's the idea.

BARNEY: Same old Joe.

JOE: Is that good or bad?

BARNEY: Both.

JOE: Same old Barney.

BARNEY: Before we get too chummy let me ask you two questions: Got any money? and Are you gonna behave?

JOE: Got money, and I've taken my meds.

BARNEY: Glad to hear it, every second drink's on the house. Four's your limit - f-o-u-r.

JOE: Got it. How about those Phillies?

BARNEY: Joe, it's not baseball season.

JOE: How about those Eagles?

BARNEY: There in last place.

JOE: The Flyers then? Those flashing blades and thunderous body checks? [Barney rolls his eyes and moves on down the bar.]

AUTHOR: Two hours and four beers later Joe would like to hang longer but Barney will have none of it.

BARNEY: You know what I said, after four you hit the door.

JOE: What are you, my probation officer? You're right, a piss and I'm gone .... after I deliver a short recitative on current events.

BARNEY: Oh fuck, here we go.

JOE: Friends, Mormons, bar flies, lend me your ears. Let's begin with the weather, or your wife: The weather's what it wants to be whether you like or not. Praise, scold, whatever, she's impossible to predict and will never ever listen or do what she's told to do. As headstrong a woman as there ever was or will be. Now, let's take the Pope: If ridiculous, antiquated accoutrements count for anything, you got to love this guy and his mystical kingdom. — Hey, you in the back, give me a break, I'm pontificating here! — All I can say is God save the little children, because that old hypocrite won't. Now let's have a go at Obama: Nice gesture, his presidency, now let's move on. People just love to hate. My on y hope is that after his

term in office, they will hate just a little less. And finally my drunken friends, us. We. All of us, Mankind. The apple has been eaten, she did it, there's no way around it. We're all fucked. And a phenomenon of greater importance, though of far less immediacy, Andromeda and the Milky Way are on a collision course. My advice? By property in another galaxy.
[A scattering of applause and boos from the few close enough to hear.]

      JOE: I'm out of here. Adios amigos.
[A scattering of "about time" and "asshole" from the patrons.]

      BARNEY: Off to a Phillies games I'll bet.

      JOE: Ya, Louie and I have box seats, you should join us sometime. There's a double-header coming up on Christmas Day, why don't you come along?

BARNEY: I'll take a snow-checkon that one. Now go Joe!

[Divertimento: A performance of the 23rd Psalm in Hebrew by the group called Brooklyn Rap Trap.]

SCENE SIX

_____

      AUTHOR: That evening, when it's just dark enough to call it night, our two vagabonds retake their position outside Stein's Jewelry Store. Their accoutrements of the night have been stored in a niche behind the building.

JOE: You know, most loyal and trusted friend, today's been a pretty good day. Plenty of sunshine, baloney of all kinds, minimal trouble, two free beers and now we're back to square one. Been fun. I wish you had a chance to hear that Mr. Jones' spiel. Scary fucking dude. And our old friend Barney, another pain in the ass. But hey man, that's just how it is, right? Right. I've got a surprise, while we were shopping for lunch I managed to lift a half pint of Beam. They really need to upgrade the security in that place. Tonight good buddy we doze off with a little warm buzz. Tomorrow maybe we'll get lucky again. Hell, I could eat baloney sandwiches until the cows come home. And there's that Lotto ticket too. Damn we're looking good.

LOUIE: Yes, I kind of agree with most of that, although I can't understand what the cows were doing away from home. I guess it could have something to do with baloney sandwiches. You've heard the expression: You're a lucky dog! Well, given the plight of many of my brothers in Third World countries, I guess I am very fortunate. I just wish Joe would find himself a woman, and take some of the pressure off of me.

AUTHOR: Before he could congratulate himself on his clever insight, Louie fell into a deep lucky-dog sleep.

[A couple of hours later.]

AUTHOR: It's now just after midnight

and Officer Clancy stops his cruiser in front of the Stein Jewelry Store and aims his spot light on our two protagonists. Neither seems disturbed by the nightly check.

OFFICER CLANCY [to himself]: There but for the grace of God go .... wait a fucking minute, who am I kidding, I haven't slept as good as those two in ten years.

AUTHOR: The officer turns off his spot and heads on into the night. Back at the jewelry store, Joe sleeps soundly, dreaming of pork chops, homemade applesauce and his high school sweetheart . Louie, equally dead to the world, dreams of pork chops, pork chops, and more pork chops. Meanwhile, at Broadway and Sixth, Officer Clancy having stopped for a red light, has fallen asleep at the wheel of his cruiser. Officer Clancy is dreaming too. He's buck naked, being chased through an apple orchard by a six hundred pound feral pig. Uneasy rests this modern day centurion.

—· CURTAIN ·—

[Immediate post-performance consensus: Seldom have so many assembled for so little. The play was over almost before it began. There were no first-nighters to query, only the cast, some of whom had not yet found their places onstage. In the confusion, someone actually did break a leg. In that sense, the production was a success.]

BACK STAGE:

Though the play has ended, the lives of its characters go on. Joe and Louie continue their daily routine. Little rain, lots of sunshine, a few bad days, but mostly good days, in the special way those two defined a good day. They did score a 10k Lotto ticket, but it didn't last long after the open bar celebration at the Sunset Tavern. For a few hours Joe was a hero. When the money ran out so did all his fans. Easy come, easy go, became Joe's mantra after that. Louie was not so philosophical in his assessment of their windfall. "How much of that manna drifted my way? A saucer of Bud Light, that's how much. Not enough for a decent buzz. Easy come, easy go? I just can't comprehend the human ethos. Everything considered though, you just have to love Joe. I sure do. But then, I haven't got a choice."

— PLAY'S END —

Albert's Head

Albert does not sleep alone. He has four plump pillows to keep him company, and ward off the demons of the night. They are always there to offer their cool side to his flushed and fretting brow. Occasionally there is a wrestling match between them, and although outnumbered four to one, Albert usually triumphs over his feathered friends who often find themselves flung to the four corners of the room. Invariably, Albert will regret his tantrum and reach down to bring his abused buddies back on board, where they again nestle together, quickly forgetting those moments spent apart and realizing they could not pass a night without each other's company. In the morning, it is with great reluctance that Albert leaves his friends. Before parting the room, he gently fluffs them up and places them just so in an anticipatory pose. All through a trying day it is with great pleasure that Albert reflects on his four friends awaiting his return and their quiet uncompromising acceptance of his weary head.

Alexander had a mind like a steel trap
— useful for catching bears, but of little
help in his urban environment. He was
encyclopedic to the point of distraction.
The score of the game was never sufficient,
there had to be an inning by inning play-by-
play. Alex was the exact opposite of terse.
He found it against his nature to summarize.
When he proposed to his wife, it went on for
over an hour. Rumor has it she accepted
just to shut him up. During the wedding
ceremony, a simple "I do." would not do.
Alex had to explain why he was saying
those words, and what those words really
meant. Although the rite was consummated,
its length thinned the guests considerably.
How she was able to abide Alex 24/7 was a
mystery to all who knew them. Helen was
quiet, quick to smile. and just a pleasant
person to be around. I was later to learn that
Helen's serious congenital hearing deficit
was the key element of their relationship.

Helen read lips, which means she has to
looking at you to understand what you're
saying. I notice Helen seldom looks at Alex.
So there you have it, a match made in
heaven. Opposites do attract and even
complement. You just never know.

Dante

Dante never asks questions, he likes to figure things out for himself. Unfortunately, he is not a gifted thinker. In fact, his mental acuity lacks an essential part — the acuity. Never-the-less, Dante has obtained a Bachelor's degree and is working on his Master's in Education. Dante believes he is going to live forever, so he's in no hurry to unravel life's mysteries which include things like algebra, Shakespeare and acronyms. Meanwhile, he imparts his singular non-invasive view of life to the sixth grade class at Lincoln Elementary School. And what do his students think of Dante's no-questions-asked approach to education? Well, they're just fine with it. "Sooner or later we'll figure it out", they unanimously agreed, "What's the big f'n hurry?"

ELMA

Elma struggled to raise herself high enough to look out the window. "What an absolutely beautiful day." she murmured, then fell back down on her pillow and closed her eyes for the last time. It was a beautiful day to live, and a beautiful day to die. On this particular occasion, Elma did both.

Going Foreword

The blank canvas awaits my pleasure.
I oblige, ravaging her purity with all
manner of color and line. When done,
we share a cigarette, that desecrated
virgin and I. As I am about to leave
the studio she asks that I lean near
and whispers this in my ear: "Good sir,
have you any idea what you've just
done?"

Gone

Suddenly she's gone. The New Yorker folded
to where she last laid eyes. Next to it, her
"I Love Vegas" mug with a quarter cup of
not yet cold black coffee. Her tooth brush
is still moist. Agitated mirrors ask, "Where is
she?" The scent deep in her pillow moans.
A longing unimaginable pervades the air. I
must return to that open magazine and finish
turning the unturned pages. In her books she
lived a thousand lives while I, in her, lived just
one. In the drama that was our life together,
she had all the best lines and was the play's
only sympathetic character. All future
performances of that production have now
been cancelled. The star is borne away.

In The Good Shepard Cemetery

In the Good Shepard Cemetery the clock
strikes, and although there are plenty of
ears here, you guessed it, none hear. A
helicopter flies low overhead and, you
guessed it, no one looks up even though
they are facing that way, not even me. So it
goes, or doesn't go, when your temperature
is way too low. No rain, no pain, no soccer
games beneath the ground, in the urns, or in
the crypts. The valley is still. I am here, lived
once but no more. Locked here in eternal
darkness with only the memories of what I
did and didn't do. I said my prayers, but,
you guessed it, that didn't really matter.
I was incinerated, didn't mind at all, as a
matter of fact I enjoyed the searing heat
— that scorching separated my body from
my soul. As before, I am still working on The
Great American novel. As before, the work
is going very slowly. Not as before, time isn't
a constraining factor. Endlessly I write and
rewrite trying to get it just right. Slowly, very
slowly, I'm beginning to realize that here,
what's right is not a constraining factor
either. It's darkness ad nauseam here in the
mausoleum. I've totally forgotten what rain
is like, or sun, or stars or loving arms. Now
the question: How can one write this great
novel with no recollection of what went
on before? That question is legitimate and
placed in the queue. In due time, I'll have
all the answers, they'll be in the Great Post-

Human American Novel, most likely in the Afterword. What time is it where you are? All of it: day, month, year. Is the sun out? How are the Dodgers doing? That's what I was afraid of — another gloomy year without a single smile or celebratory cheer.

***

IT SNOWED LAST NIGHT

It snowed last night. Someone died last night. That's pretty much all the news. The flat-screen told me so. I like news channels, French fries, Budweiser, guns of a high caliber, women of a low caliber, and Jesus Christ the Almighty. That's pretty much who I am — the forgotten American. Now, unless you brought your own beer, go on, get the hell out of here!

When Mary wed she foresaw a life full of kids and contentment. Six months in, and five months pregnant, the man of her dreams left her this note: "Seeking true happiness. It's not you, it's me." Life Plan #1 lay in tatters. When little Jimmy was born with Downs, there went Plan #2. It was as if the marital cruise ship had sunk. She had a life vest, but young Jimmy did not. Her mother's instinct kept them both afloat, but from deep in the sea, there were murmurs of: Just let go. On an overcast day in late May, Mary and little Jimmy had their last meal: a hand full of little white pills. Carefully, Mary laid her child down, then took her place beside him. There their lives ended. Plan #3 had gone without a hitch. At the gravesite, the preacher droned on about the mystery of God's ways, and how these two were now in a world without pain. Post mortem, Mary rolled her eyes at the prospect of what she had tried so hard to avoid — the eternally revolving door of Plan #4.

My Guide

My guide is the TV Guide. My life is
meaningless without it. Am I embarrassed
to admit it? No, I have a plan, that's it, and
I stick to it. Hey, It works for me. Structure
is essential. How about you, got a plan
detailed to the quarter hour? I doubt it.
Perfect? No, the guide is not perfect, what
is. The frequency of commercial messages
is a problem. There's always bad with
the good, how else can you make the
distinction. Every life needs a guide. What
are you doing next Thursday night at eight
fifteen? I rest my case.

MEATLOAF

Marge frequently makes meatloaf for supper, and Marge's meatloaf has a wide following. Those meals needed no celebration to be served. To the diners, Marge's piece de resistance was reason enough to celebrate. After these meals, participants often lingered on into the evening exchanging anecdotes and generally reveling in their after-dinner haze. Marge's secret meatloaf recipe was just that. That piece of gastronomic alchemy help keep the family together. Without it, she might find herself out of the loop. Nothing dispelled animosity or loneliness like one of those special meals at Marge's. Some think Marge an eccentric. Rumor has it she does her gardening in the cellar. There, she is purported to tenderly care for, amidst a 24 hour glare, the exotic herb that makes her specialty so special. Whether these rumors are true or not I cannot say. All I can attest to is this: No matter how knotted your mental state, when you pushed your chair away from her table, you and all the guests who partook of Marge's magic cookery, wore what came to be known as "the meatloaf grin".

Recipe for Marge's Meatloaf:

- 1 cup of finely chopped onion
- 1 celery rib, chopped fine
- 1 Tbsp minced garlic
- 1 carrot, chopped fine
- 1/2 cup of finely chopped scallions
- 2 Tbsp unsalted butter
- 2 teaspoon salt
- 1 1/2 tsp freshly ground pepper
- 2 tsp Worcestershire sauce
- 2/3 cup ketchup
- 1 1/2 pounds of ground chuck
- 3/4 pound of spicy ground pork sausage
- 1 cup fresh bread crumbs
- 2 large eggs, beaten slightly
- 1 cup minced fresh "mystery herb"

Have a sip of wine then combine. Another sip or two then into the oven with you. 350° for an hour and it should be done, and if you're still sipping, you too should be done.

NORMAL:

Usual, common, standard, average,
natural, regular, ordinary, acknowledged,
typical, conventional, routine, accustomed,
habitual, run-of-the-ill.

ABOUT NORMAL:

They tell me I'm normal — what I'm always
hoping not to hear. Every test I take
reinforces this conclusion. Body temp:
About normal. Heart rate: About normal.
Rorschach test: About normal. Penis size:
About normal. Back pain: Normal for a man
your age. Anxiety: Normal for a man your
age with back-pain. Depression: Normal
for a man your age and background.
Impotence: Normal for a man of your
age with anxiety and depression. Suicidal
Thoughts: Normal for a man with back pain,
anxiety, depression and impotence. "Does
it help you in any way to know you are
the very definition of normal?" Well no, I'd
like to think that there is something about
me that is not normal, that sets me apart,
that makes me, let's say, abnormal. "I can
assure you that your desire to be abnormal is
understandable, predictable and perfectly
normal."

No Drama Here

The Pelican Bay Country Club was where the million dollar wedding and reception were held. He twenty-four, she twenty-three. He: a degree in real estate management, she: Urban Planning. He worked in his dad's firm, she in her dad's. (No, not a taste of the sour grapes here.) They honeymooned in the South Pacific while their thirty-five hundred squared foot Newport Coast Home was being finished.   Sounds perfect, looked perfect, was perfect, and one year in, still perfect. Now I know what you're waiting for: How their idyllic lives became polluted, proving money cannot buy happiness and often destroys it. Right? Well, you're wrong. In this particular case, wealth and privilege were no impediment to happiness — they augmented it. It is now ten years hence, the two are now a family of four, and all is well, and is likely to remain so for the foreseeable future. There just is no drama here, or, if you like, the drama here is the lack of it. What can I say? You just never know.

Not Again

Michael woke up with a nearly incapacitating hangover. No matter the pain, he showered and dressed for work. I've got to go in. I've taken up every inch of slack given me. Somewhere between his garage and the office, Michael lost control of the car and ended up parked in front of Paul's Bar which just happens to: OPEN AT 6AM. Not again, Paul thought to himself, not again. I just can't keep doing this. He found an open spot at the bar and ordered a double shot of vodka. The bar tender was sympathetic to his plight and poured to the surface tension's limit. Paul rested his forearms on the bar and slid his hands over to steady the glass. He then lowered his lips down and sucked off the first quarter inch of vodka without spilling a drop. A notable achievement thought he, for someone in my condition. Then with elbows still resting on the bar he tilted the glass up with both hands and managed to empty it. Finally, fuel for the waning embers of my aching soul, he muttered. Michael sat staring at that empty shot glass for maybe an hour, refusing several offers of a refill. Then Michael got up and walked out, went on to work and managed to finish the day without incident. Something happened to Michael that day. In one singular moment of that mysterious day — he walked away — and Michael has not been back since. Shit happens, or doesn't happen. Do you decide, or is it decided for you? You just never know.

I really mean it

I hate my brother, he's younger and sickly and gets all the attention. How about me family? I've got pimples, big stinky feet, and sneakers that are not even last year's model. I am forced to carry my lunch in a brown paper bag that reeks of egg salad. This requires that I eat my lunch on the way to school to avoid being pilloried. It's always little Jimmy this and little Jimmy that. I'm sick of it. I'm going to run away, I swear, unless I get some respect. I'll live on Hollywood Boulevard and let all kinds of weird guys do all kinds of weird shit to me for money. Hey mom, look at me now, getting fucked in the ass for a living. Cry mom, cry. Your first born has gone astray, and do you know whose fault it is? It's Jimmy's fault, and yours too. I hate you both. Take that God-fearing family! And, as the Lord is my witness, this time I really, really, really, mean it!

One Lucky Hombre

Juan had stopped his Cushman motor scooter for the red light at Wilshire and Barrington. It was cnother beautiful Friday morning in Southern California and Juan was thinking ahead to the weekend in Tijuana when he heard the screeching brakes. Juan tensed and waitec. When Juan awakened, he had been in the hospital for three days. He was busted up pretty good, but the doctor's assured him that against all odds, he was going to be able to live a normal life given the advances in prosthetic devices. Wow, thought Juan, I'm one lucky hombre! Apparently, Juan clso suffered some serious head trauma. You just never know. (Nor will he.)

SWEET ROSE

Sweet Rosie had four impudent kids and one abusive husband. How she kept it together no one knew. She lived for a few hours of peace in the middle of the night. Breast cancer came at fifty-one, death at fifty-three. "Thank you Jesus!" was Rose's parting murmur. "Now please, turn off that infernal eternal light and let me get some sleep."

The Great Muse in the twelve hundred dollar shoes paid me another visit this morning. About 5am it was, just as the sun rose. I dread those encounters. He orates with great bluster and will breach no interruption. On and on: What I did and didn't do, what I should and shouldn't do, all in mortifying detail. He knows things about me I haven't even done yet. When the rebuke ends, he asks for questions. I never have any. Why bother, he knows it all. That's what makes these encounters so painful. He's always right — and for a guy with my kind of problems, omniscience is last thing you need to face at five o'clock in the morning.

The Dressing Room

I hate trying on clothes in the store dressing room. For me, it's an awkward struggle. I'd rather take the garment home, then if it doesn't fit take it back. Once, late in the afternoon, about an hour before Macy's was about to close, in a struggle to try on a pair of Jeans, I fell and hit my head. When I came too, the store was closed and dark. I sat up for a few minutes to clear the cobwebs and get my bearings, then headed for an exit. I must have set off alarms of some kind because before I knew it I was sitting in the back of a patrol car. Eventually, they believed my story and let me go. Funny thing though, I was still wearing that pair of Jeans that tripped me up, and I hadn't paid for. So, I guess you would think everything turned out OK, which is not the case because the pants I went into the store wearing were left hanging in the dressing room along with my wallet containing $80 in cash and all my credit cards. It was a big hassle, but I finally got it all squared away. The only real downside to this adventure was the bump on my forehead, and the fact that the Jeans I got away with didn't fit and I had to return them for store credit because I didn't have a receipt, which makes sense seeing how I never really bought them in the first place. Anyway, now maybe you can understand why I hate to try on stuff in those little cubicles where just about anything can happen. You just never know.

The Greening Of A Boy

When I was a young boy, a very long time
ago, I saw with my own eyes a frog swallow
a big fat slow flying green fly. Then, even
at my tender age I was aware of the two
things most closely associated with the fly:
shit and maggots. Though only seven years
old at the time, I had this innate skill for
making moral judgments. I judged the fly
not at fault for doing the disgusting things
he was programmed to do. Now the frog
on the other hand, had a choice. There
were plenty other food sources around, but
he chose, I repeat chose, of his own free
will, to eat that winged purveyor of disgust.
I could not, and to this day cannot, forgive
so vile a moral gastronomic transgression.
As a matter of fact, I'm still repelled by
things that are green-spotted, croak,
and hop. I recently broke off my one and
only engagement because my fiancé, a
country girl, exhibited some of those same
characteristics. I guess my points are these:
First: Our likes and dislikes are determined
very early on, and Second: One must never,
no matter how aroused one becomes, kiss a
frog on the mouth.

The Walnut Tree

My older brother Jimmy lived in the walnut tree. Well, almost. He spent as much time up there as our parents would allow. In the upper branches of that tree Jimmy suspended himself between heaven and earth. Up there, he thought himself very close to heaven with free food, things with wings and a great view of the planet earth below. You might be surprised to know that at the time Jimmy was not a kid, not in the physical sense, but a twenty-three year old. You're no more surprised than I, when I stop to remember him. When the walnuts were in their season, Jimmy and the crows engaged in great aerial battles over the rights to the nuts. The crow squadron was led by the infamous Black Baron and in opposition, was Jimmy, alone in his Sopwith Camel . Oh how the nuts flew in those tree-top battles. In fact, Jimmy and his adversaries were really good friends. A one-sided relationship for sure, because Jimmy was no match for those clever and mischievous black birds. Still, they enjoyed each other's company, as fellow aviators often do. And even if Jimmy suspected they didn't take him seriously, he didn't let on. So it went around home, the giant man-child aviator (Jimmy wasn't a little guy at six foot three and 230 pounds.) high up in the walnut tree shouting "Look out below!" and "Bombs away!" to anyone man or beast who happens to come near.

"Jimmy boy, come on down from that tree, it's lunch time." Mom would call. "Jimmy, come on down from that goddamned tree, it's supper time you nut." Dad would yell. I could never figure out whether Dad was trying to be funny or cruel. No matter, Jimmy loved to eat almost as much as he liked to perch in the walnut tree. And, battle-weary though he was, he could get from tree-top to table top in the blink of an eye. There were some who believed Jimmy could fly. "Jimmy, God blame it, take off those goggles at the table." "Yes sir!" was Jimmy's military like reply. I don't really think Dad ever forgave Jimmy for what happened to his old mare Dottie. He loved that old gal so. Anyway, Jimmy was cleaning up in the barn one morning and somehow Dottie got spooked by something and gave a kick that just missed Jimmy's head. Well, Jimmy kind of lost his temper and kicked back. I told you how Jimmy was a big kid, well, when Jimmy kicked back he didn't miss, and old Dottie was hurt so bad she had to be put down. Kind of a different take on the man bites dog thing. Afterwards, Jimmy spent more time than ever up the walnut tree, and Dad stopped trying to divert him with odd jobs. Hell, Dad even stopped calling him down for supper. Early in the Fall of my junior year in college I got a frantic phone call from my mother that something had happened to Jimmy and they needed me home right away. Nothing to worry

about she said, we just need you home for
a while. It was strange driving up to the
house and not seeing Jimmy semaphoring
a hello from up the old walnut tree. Seems
Jimmy's weight had worked against him as
he was firing his prop-synchronized machine
gun, the branch he was standing on gave
way and Jimmy plunged straight down
into the ground. He had been too low for
his parachute to deploy. Jimmy's back
was broke as clean as the branch he was
standing on. There was nothing I, or anyone
could do. Thereafter, Mom would wheel
Jimmy out under the canopy from which
he fell, and he'd stay there as long as Mom
could stand watching him stare up from the
world he so often looked down upon. Sure
the crows were still around, although they
no longer taunted, and seemed to defer to
him. Mom reported seeing crows dropping
walnuts right into his lap. In August of the
summer after I graduated from college, I
took a peanut butter and jelly sandwich and
a glass of cold milk out to Jimmy, but Jimmy
did not respond. Jimmy had flown away. I
slumped in my chair as Jimmy was slumped
in his, and cried for a long time before going
back into the house with the news. We
buried Jimmy as close to that walnut tree
as its roots would allow. Mom cried for the
longest time. Dad, I just don't know how he
felt. If he felt anything it didn't show. "God's
will', he muttered now and again, "An eye
for an eye." It's been a long time since those

days. Mom and Dad have passed, and I sold the farm to a young family from the city. But the walnut tree is still there, looking rather gnarly but ever vigilant in shading Jimmy's marker beneath it. Funny thing though, there aren't any crows around. I guess now, out of respect for their ate adversary, the old walnut tree with Jimmy entangled in its roots, has been designated a no-crow fly zone.

***

What Lousy Luck

Old Jesse sat waiting for the 87A City Lines bus as he has done for thirty some years. Sometimes it arrives a little early, sometime a little late, but it has never been this late. Thirty minutes now he's been waiting and is getting a little annoyed.

[Jump back to forty minutes ago and two miles away.]

Fred's been a City Lines bus driver for a long time and he's never had an accident, 'til now. Fred doesn't know where he came from. There was this flash of red out of the corner of his eye, then two stocking feet in front of the windshield. Oh God, the unimaginable has happened to that poor little boy, to his parents, and to me.

[Jump ahead to now]

Old Jesse is getting more stressed out by the minute. For sure he's missed the start of the Bingo tournament at the Senior Center. Jesus H Christ, muttered Jesse to himself, what lousy luck. I wonder what's going to happen next? You just never know.

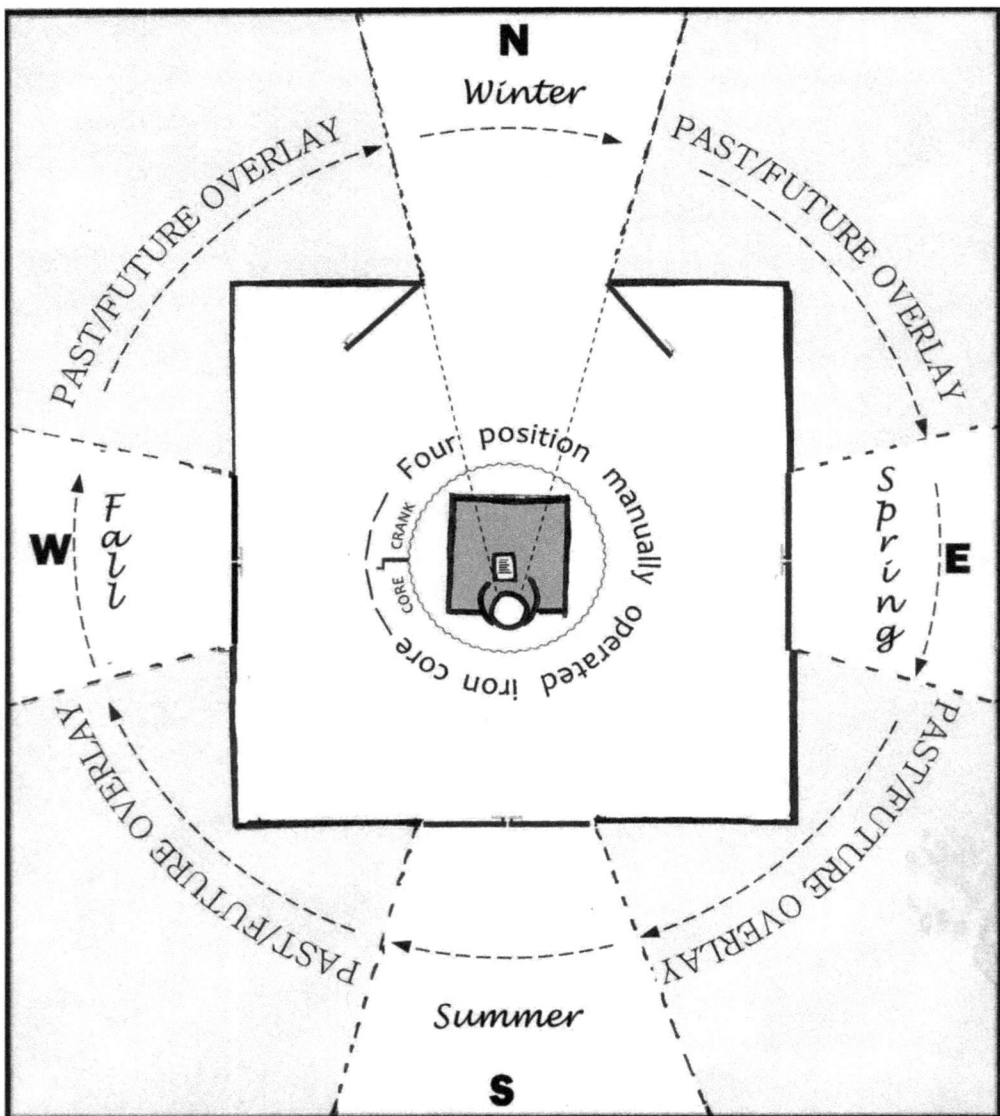

N
Winter

PAST/FUTURE OVERLAY

PAST/FUTURE OVERLAY

Four position manually operated iron core

CORE CRANK

W
Fall

E
Spring

PAST/FUTURE OVERLAY

PAST/FUTURE OVERLAY

Summer

S

FOREWARD

Incredible as it might seem, there are those
who lead full, painless, happy, productive
lives and die in old age surrounded by those
they love, which just happen to be those
who love them. Its SRO at the memorial
services. In direct opposition to them are the
residents of Nadir Arms. We will be visiting
some of them; and if you're not interested in
the imperfect man, stop here and read no
further. I have had the dubious distinction
of being a resident of The Arms, and my
empathy for those interned there is genuine.
In fact, I get offers of complimentary rooms
all the time. For a long time now, I have
been able to decline those offers. My visit
this time is in a official capacity — as Artist
in Residence. The 6th Floor is the artist's loft.
And, there is no loft less lofty than the loft at
The Nadir Arms.

There's an old hotel downtown wherein reside people down, try desperately each day to rise up. Long gray linoleum clad halls, with institutional-green walls. Flickering sixty watt bulbs add an anthracite-like aura. Crooked numbers hang tenuously on reluctant doors, mysteriously bolted from within and without. Open transoms expel the sounds and smells of isolation cells. A chorus of grunting and groaning rise from prostrate forms attempting resurrection and interruption of the dream always dreamed: a far off place of distorted half familiar images, and a single all-consuming imperative — find the way home. *Sir, can you help me? Is this the bus that takes me home? Pardon me sir, can you help me, I've forgotten my way home.*

It's late at night, the figure in 303 is spread out on her khaki spread. Ceiling cracks look down at her, while she returns the stare, eyes ever upward trying to connect the fractured lines of a starless plaster sky. "I live only for fear of dying. On some inclement day, from this roof 's ledge I'll fly, guaranteeing the remembrance of me in the nightmares of those few obliged to sweep me form the avenue." Not everyone feels this degree of desperation. To some, The Nadir Arms is a way station on the journey home — the ticket that can only be purchased with self-forgiveness. So come along, we'll visit The Arms that both cradle and discard.

THE LAYOUT:
Six floors, roof and basement.
1st floor – Rooms for the infirm and acrophobic.
Meeting room and cafeteria.
2nd floor – Women deemed salvageable.
3rd floor – Women deemed unsalvageable (trash).
4th floor – Salvageable men.
5th floor – Male throwaways, homosexuals and republicans.
6th floor - Resident Artist's loft. (The Venthouse.)
Roof - Tanning salon (When the sun is shining.), no swimming pool, but there is a very popular diving board.
Cellar – Furnace, washers, dryers, building super's cave, lost and found locker and a crematorium (currently down for repairs).
Room furnishing: single bed with one pillow and a khaki spread, chest of drawers – some with knobs, understuffed chair, lamp table, lamp with 40wt bulb, card table and two folding chairs, and a pot to piss in. Roomers are allowed to add certain items — like a TV for instance, no larger than 19 inches please. The forementioned pot is provided free of charge in case the occupant doesn't want to disturb their neighbors by flushing at night; and secondly, to invalidate any claim made

by the resident that he or she "Hasn't got a pot to piss in."

List of some item currently in Lost & Found: A Frisbee missing its bee, a single red suspender, a hazel glass eye that's winks while you're looking the other way, various artificial limbs tangled in obscene positions , a Boston Braves baseball cap, sun glass for a monocle, EEEE cup bra or a parachute (not sure which), one Nike size 16EEE running shoe (you could put both feet in it and hop), and an old dude claiming to be Moses. Items are kept for ninety days then disposed of, except for Moses. (Nobody seems to want this guy.)

THE STAFF:
There is other part time help that come and go, but these are the principal players.
Hotel Manager — ELVIS HILTON
Elvis had connections in the hotel business and a bright future until he got on the wrong side of both the Mob and LAPD. By skimming drug and prostitution money he lost the advantage his family name gave him, along with the thumb on his left hand. Elvis is grateful to have this job, and his life. Likely, it was his name that saved him. Elvis dresses impeccably, and although he bares no resemblance to that other Elvis, he does sport one hell-of-a pompadour.
"Good morning gentlemen. Welcome to Nadir Arms, how can I assist you?"

Elevator Operator: OTIS DOWNS
Open, close, up down, good morning,
good afternoon, good luck. Everybody
knows Otis, Otis knows everybody — but not
really. He probably hasn't had a sustained
conversation with any of his riders in 15
years. People just don't' talk much on
elevators, which is fine with Otis, because
he doesn't have much to say inside the lift
or out. He often reminds himself that Lyndon
Johnson was once an elevator operator
in San Bernardino; and although he has
no political aspirations, his endeavor does
have its successes. Besides that, elevator
operators are an endangered species, but
there's no organized effort to save them
from extinction. Some say Otis is already
extinct. He's heard this remark and wonders
how anybody living in this dump could throw
such weighty stones. "Good morning, going
up."

Security: RICHARD TRACY
Richard (he prefers Richard) is a retired LAPD
officer. After 21 years of service he was shot
in the foot by a trainee and was forced to
a take a disability retirement. Policing Nadir
Arms keeps him or his toes, so to speak.
Richard tries at all times to be fair, firm and
friendly, and it works— just like out on the
street, most of the time. He finds most of the
anger here is directed inward. If someone
turns up with a knot on their head, it's likely
they've been banging their own head

against a wall. Richard still earnestly believes his job is to serve and protect. Even the most paranoid of Nadir Arms residents feel safer when Mr. Tracy's around. "Hello Sarah, I've gotten a report you've been banging on the walls of your room in the wee hours."

Doorman: CONRAD
Conrad doesn't work for the hotel. Nadir Arms has no doorman. Conrad is so often propped in the doorway that residents and locals alike have given him the title by default. Conrad the Doorman has no schedule — no work schedule, no life schedule. Conrad's part of what makes The Arms and environs so ... well, how shall I say it — horizontal.
"Good Morning Conrad. It's OK, don't get up, I've got it."

Maintenance: MANNY THE MOLE
Manny the janitor lives down below, as far down as the elevator will go, down with the rusting pipes, hissing boilers and the heavy odor of mildew mixed with a hint of methane gas. Manny's not the only one living down here, but he is the only one that walks on two legs. For thirty-two years he has called this dungeon home. Manny has heard it all, seen it all, been a part of it all: Scrubbed brain splatter from the walls, cleared toilets plugged with fetuses, mopped up thick dark pools of blood, and all the time trying to remain above it all

down below it all. There are those who'll say he has failed to separate himself from what he does.

Visit me any time, says Manny the Mole, just give me time to dig you a hole. Ha Ha Ha, goes Manny, the droll Mole of Nadir Arms.

Room 120 — GRACIE
Gracie's life was playing out like a one act romantic comedy, that is until her husband had a heart attack and died on Sunday morning at 4am PST. After the shroud dropped on Act One, it became clear to her this play was to have more than one act. From the very first lines of Act Two, at 4:01 PST, what had started as a light-hearted melodrama was quickly turning into a tragic farce. Gracie's husband mishandled the finances. The family's lifestyle had been over-leveraged. Second mortgage, third mortgage, unpaid life insurance premiums, maxed out credit cards. Act Two ended with Gracie on the street drinking 99c bottles of Muscatel through a straw to make time flow more quickly and the wine more slowly. Yet, there is a stubbornness deep inside our protagonist that will not let her accept a performance limited to just two acts.
The Third Act opened in Room 120 of The Nadir Arms.

Room 206 — PHOEBE
All together, Phoebe has had parts in maybe fifty movies and TV shows. Her face

is familiar to many, but they're never certain where to place it. She's been out of work now for more than ten years. Too much time between jobs, too much booze. The next thing she knew, her ball of cashmere yarn had unraveled. A.A. has gotten her to The Arms. Once she has a year or so of sobriety, she'll begin knocking on once familiar doors and perhaps reignite her acting career. Till then, she'll breathe deeply and live it one day at a time. "Hello, my name is Phoebe and I'm an alcoholic. I've been sober now for 30 days." [Applause.]

Room 212 —JANIS
Late of South Carolina, Janis came to L.A. two years ago to flutter her lashes, wiggle her ass and make those in "the business" take notice. They did indeed, except it wasn't the kind of attention she imagined. Those purporting to be in "the business" wanted auditions alright, but the parts all involved dancing — lap dancing, and close-ups— of her giving head. Janis soon found she performed best and thought less when she was stoned. Eventually, the only way she could stay stoned was to lap-dance and give head. In just two years, L.A. had brought the adorable little southern girl to her knees — literally. A rescue mission found her this spot. For Janis, Nadir Arms is a way up, and hopefully a way out of L.A. It appears Janis has finally been discovered — by Janis. "Hi, my name is Janis and I'm a

grateful addict."

Room 308 — CASSIDY
*Four kids and five grandkids and none of
them worth a shit. I haven't heard a word
from any of them in 3 years; not a post card,
not a how are you, or a fuck you. So I made
a few mistakes, so fucking what.* Such is the
mindset of Cassidy, the occupant of Room
308. A West Virginia Coal miner's daughter
who by the time she was fourteen had been
fucked by most of the male members of her
family. The expression "damaged goods"
could have been invented to describe
Cassidy. Most examining the extent of the
damage to this young woman might write
in the space provided for condition —
Totaled! By twenty she had four kids and
two husbands. Who the fathers were of her
four children would require DNA testing.
Cassidy's is now thirty-eight, looks twice
that, and persists by stringing one day to the
other with the help of a crack pipe. She's on
another program now, and tries, she really
tries. When she looks in a mirror, she wonders
why she's trying. Cassidy is tired, very tired.
And those she's left behind? *Like I said, fuck
them all. I'm just too goddamned tired to
care.* "Hey, you guys got any ... you know
... stuff? You could hang out and we could
do all sorts of ... you know ... stuff." No thanks
Cassidy, maybe some other time.
Assholes!

Room 303 — SARAH
Sarah was a stay-at-home mom. Her
husband had a great job, and she and
he and the three kids had everything they
needed and a lot they didn't. Living on
the West Side and considering themselves
hip, they did all the hip things the hip
people were doing. This lifestyle mandated
weekend parties that offered a candy store
of chemical catalysts. Sarah's catalyst of
choice was the tequila-cocaine cocktail:
chase a line of coke with a double shot of
tequila. Life was good, but not 24 hours a
day. Making it so became Sarah's raison
d'être. Thus the downward spiral began. As
the laws of motion dictate, the further down
the faster the spin until most of what was
Sarah had spun away, leaving a hollow core
with a faintly beating heart. That's the Sarah
we find staring at the ceiling of Nadir Arms
There's a knocking at the door; the social
worker has come to check on her. A very
faint *Come in*. How are you Sarah? Stay
positive Sarah, you must not give up on
yourself! *Sure*, came the heartless response,
sure.

Room 407 — MARK
Those burns on his arms? Mark saved two
people's lives by pulling them out of a
burning car that was rear-ended at 80MPH
by a drunk driver on the i10. The baby in the
back seat he did not see and was burned

to death. Mark then pulled the drunk out of the other car and proceeded to beat him to death with a lug wrench he found laying in the street. Mark got five years for manslaughter, served 18 months and was assigned Nadir Arms as part of his probation. Does Mark have regrets? He does, for going after the ass-hole that caused the accident. Had he not been so bent on vengeance perhaps, just perhaps, he might have done a more thorough search of that burning car. Mark, any plans for the future? That shouldn't be a problem. I'm a hero you know, a big fucking hero. *IRENE's in the hall crying. Hear that? it's coming from the 3rd Floor, it's Irene in the hall crying. Irene loves to hear herself crying there; her sobbing is even more compelling, a plaintive barely human echoing. Fact is, I like it too. Often I'll pause and listen for a while, makes my spine tingle, my eyes tear up. Cry Irene, keep crying on the third floor, in the long green hall, it helps us all Irene, to hear you bawl.*

Room 409 — MATTHEW
Matt was a Junior high math and science teacher for twelve years, until hands-on research into the anatomy of a 14 year old female got him jail time and the resume killing appellation SEX OFFENDER. Matt had no previous record, and to that point was the model husband and father. So much for modeling. Part of his probation has placed him at Nadir Arms. Matt felt sure the judge

got a perverse pleasure in assigning him to a place so named. Matthew is determined to pay his debt and move on. Maybe go down South somewhere and start over; maybe work with senior citizens. "Good Evening, my name is Matthew and I'm a pedophile."

Room 404 — PHILLIP
Phillip likes it here. Phil has no chemical dependency problems except for Colgate tooth paste and coffee. Phillip looks happy. Shit, Phillip is happy. He loves sitting around with the guys listening to their tales of crime and punishment turned comic opera. Phil lives those experiences vicariously, allowing him to wake up every morning without a hangover and free of regret. Phil's a listener, and everyone likes a listener. Unfortunately, Phil does nothing else. Phil is not part of any group he hangs with, he is the group, with no individual identity. The group is Phillip's life raft. Without it, he would like sink completely out of sight. As long as he can attend a conversation between two or more people, Phillip will be fine. If Phillip was isolated, it wouldn't be long before he'd be seeking the eternal spring of the Nadir Arms rooftop diving board. *You fellas want some company? I could just hang with you, I wouldn't say a word.*
Sorry Phillip, but we're just about to leave, maybe some other time.

Room 502 — RALPH
For Twenty-seven years Ralph drove a L.A.
city bus. Hell, everybody that didn't have a
car in the center of town knew him. Twice
driver of the year, he was Mr. RTD. Then
strange shit started to happen. Like he'd
collect no fares for an entire day, or he
wouldn't stop when the bell rang, or stop
at a corner where no one was waiting and
honk, or come to work in pajamas and
slippers. Well, needless to say, in a town
like L.A., noted for its excellence in public
transportation, this erratic behavior could
not be tolerated. Ralph had to go, and he
went — from bus stop bench to bus stop
bench, and in and out of jail for all manner
of petty transgressions. Once he climbed
on top of a bus and road around spread-
eagled for half a day before a helicopter
pilot spotted him and the fire department
managed to get him down. Thanks to an
effort by a group of ex-passengers he got a
room at The Arms. He was not a happy man,
he used to be but no more. Now Ralph is,
well, the closest I can come is bewildered.
Ralph is a bewildered man. [Knock, knock.]
Hey Ralph can we come in? *No, I'm not
here!* We believe him, and move on.

Room 509 — REMBRANDT
Rembrandt, aka The Artist, is a thief, and has
been one as long as he can remember. He
is good at it, and being good at it meant
he never had to be good at anything else.

When he was nine he had more walkin-around-money in his pocket than his dad made in a week. He caught a lot of breaks because he was so young, cute, smart and polite. As he got older this shine wore off. By the time The Artist was 21, he had spent half his teens in Juvenile detention, and done two years of hard time. Still there were those in the hood who had not given up on him, as his parents had years before. Catholic services had arranged for him to stay at The Arms while serving his probation. Even the few supporters he had felt that this was likely his final chance at salvation. What did Rembrandt think? He saw this as a great opportunity to get back his groove. An honest living is a concept he had never grasped. *Believe this*, he told us, *the next score will be major — one major fucking score. Remember where you heard it. And by the way, don't you guys have anything better to do — like cheating on your taxes or something? Give me a break, I've got plans to make.*

Loft Studio The Penthouse
Here resides The Oracle of Nadir Arms. A commission awarded every once in a while to an artist who is challenged to illuminate those domiciled beneath him, *The Unsuccessful Ones,* who are undetectable on radar, yet occupy a greater life-space than most of us. There's a desk situated on a revolving platform that can be cranked

into any one of four positions: North, South, East and West. In the center of each corresponding wall are windows looking out. To the north forever the winter's sky, To the south lingers the longest day Eastward the questions spring to life, Westward the answers fall. The writer merely chooses his season, cranks the handle revolving the platform to one of the four positions. Beware the Past/Future overlays! These are areas beyond the artist's ability to see — the blind spots. As you can plainly see, there's more to life than meets even the most poetic eye, unless you lie. Looking: Northward is the ever warming present. Northward I spy: Valley girls, Mount Wilson revealing the ever expanding sky. Mount Shasta's runoff running off to quench thirsts and fill swimming pools five hundred miles away in arid L.A. And there's Elliot Bay, the North Slope, Polar Bears, darkness, Northern lights, and the melting ice. Southward circumscribes today as an arching summer sun moves away, casting its shadow on the Orange County Line, drawn in the sand with rhinestones. Families circumventing border fencing, trembling millions in Mexico City. Panama with its very own canal. Cocoa leaves, and ever shrinking hardwood trees with the Amazon running fearlessly through. Patagonia, Cape Horn, and Emperor Penguins too. And beneath it all the melting ice. Looking East I see the past: with thunderous herds of buffalo,

autonomous tribes of Native Americans
from sea to shining sea. Rows of dead at
Gettysburg, Pilgrims disembarking where
Vikings had centuries before. Great sheets
of ice gouging lakes and falls. That, and all
that's past lies there before me, to the East.
Westward lies the unsettling future, right
out there, close enough to smell, taste and
feel, playing out before me: Multicultural
L.A. suspended above the deepest deep
blue sea. Hawaii Islands procreating still.
Asia, rising from hibernation. Opium to
ease the white man's pain. And oh yes,
there's Shangri-La, which to those like me,
is Los Angeles on a clear day in December
when one can see the future unrestrained,
trampling over convention in shorts, flip-flops
and a tank top to the beat of hip-hop.

OK, seen enough? Lets go down. Hey Otis,
why the frown? Of course we're going
down.There's only one other way out, right?
No, no, just to the first floor, my visitor's done.
Hey Elvis, my friend here thanks you for your
hospitality. Thanks but no thanks Elvis, he's
got a place to stay. Stay right there Conrad,
we've got the door. Well my friend, come
any time, I'll be here till Christmas.

***

Late-breaking Nadir Arms news items:

Phillis Miller, oft time Nadir Arms resident, miscarried a bouncing baby boy last Wednesday. The tyke bounced all the way to the dump in the back of a trash truck.

Big Lisa Malloy, who volunteers in the kitchen, was hit by a Mini-Cooper while crossing Broadway last week. Lisa's just fine, but the Mini sustained major damage (totalled).

Reminder: Thursday lunch special features sauerkraut and wieners with lime and carrot jello for desert. Max Plank will be playing his accordion. Wunderbar!

Gilbert and Armando were caught together in the 4th floor storage room. Details are sketchy — something to do with a plunger and a mop handle.

Remember to worship on Sundays. You owe him.

Cleveland

I have just purchased a cow's tongue.
Wrapped neatly in butcher paper I place
the package next to me and start home.
I decide on a circuitous route because
how often does one get to drive around
Cleveland in a 1959 Dodge with a cow's
tongue in the passenger's seat. It's very
likely this has never happened before in the
history of Cleveland, or not at least since
1959. How singular that tongue, the Dodge
and me. For some reason I feel very proud
that this is happening to me, and that it's
happening in Cleveland.

Buck Rogers

Buck Rogers sat a few stools down bemoaning his rocket pack's failure to pass the California emissions test. He was grounded. Good thing too, 'cause he was pretty much on his ass. Too much rocket fuel I guess. It's comforting to see our heroes are more or less just like us. "Hey Buck, let me buy you a drink." When I left he was teetering. Soon after, he was to crash and burn, rocket pack and all. The next morning Buck shook off the effects of his crash, donned the hero's accoutrements, minus the rocker pack, and set off for the bus stop. Buck felt no indignity in having to wait there with ordinary mortals – it was the blinding sun he couldn't bear. If you've ever had a rocket fuel hangover, then you'll appreciate Buck's pain. That very next day, Buck began work on a solar powered propulsion pack.

Design-a-Tot

Kristen and Matthew agreed – it was time
to expand the family. They also agreed
the third member was to be a boy. So they
went online to Design-a-Tot and filled out
the obligatory forms as to their preferences:
hair color, disposition, skin color – almond
was popular, height, mental capacity –
no dunce, but no eccentric genius either.
There were over 2000 mental and physical
characteristics to choose from. Kristen and
Matthew agreed, they wanted no surprises.
9 months later, the text message came:
"Your baby's ready!" That evening after
work they stopped by the distribution center.
There were no surprises wrapped in the little
blue blanket. They both agreed the initial
sensation of parenthood was very close to
what they felt a year before when they took
delivery of their new BMW 535 Sedan. They
figured the monthly costs would be about
the same too.

Down Below

I'm a stoker, I make this vessel go.
Close to hell I am — down below.
Each day I come topside to see
if the sky's where it ought to be;
then, reassured , I descend below.
Fires rage there, oh Lord the heat there.
No earthly fire except your funeral pyre will
ever burn so — down below. I sleep there, in
black heat I sleep, praying my soul to keep,
if I die before I wake, Please Lord, more heat
I cannot take.

Ellen

Ellen could not believe something so big
would fit into her; or later, something that
large could come out of her. She smiles
while others weep, and weeps when others
smile. Ellen could never understand the
rules of engagement, or disengagement.
She often wonders why some cheeses have
holes in them while others do not. She's
afraid to ask someone for fear they'll think
she's stupid. Ellen is not stupid. Her mother
told her that a long time ago. ventilated
cheese is just another of life's mysteries. Ellen
may not know it, but she is a far greater
mystery than cheese of any shape or form –
or even elbow macaroni for that matter.

Fit as a Fiddle

I'm fit as a fiddle, yet I can't resist parking in those spaces reserved for the handicapped. Fuck those people. Most of them were told by their doctors to get plenty of exercise. So you see, I'm helping. That's me, a bleeding heart rebel. I'm a careful driver, but, if there's no opposing traffic, I'll just blow that stop sign. And, you know that signal late at night that has you stopped for no reason? I'll blow that too. That's me, the iconoclast, breaking all the rules. I once jerked off during Sunday mass, even getting a drop or two ejaculate on the braid of the woman sitting in front of me. Now that's some wild shit. Yes, I'm one reckless motherfucker. That stunt in the church did not go unnoticed. After the service Father Phil took me aside and said he'd like to see me that evening in his quarters. I obliged, what the fuck is he going to say. Well, he explained that in front of the altar was not the place to get off, and if I had impulses like that again I'd be more than welcome to come to his quarters, and he would be more than happy to assist in any way he could. Well, all I can say is, I found a soul mate. That Father Phil is as wild and fucked up as I am. Amen.

Just A Quarter Block from Home

Evelyn Anne Moskowitz was halfway across the grocery store parking lot when lightening stuck her down. Just a quarter block from home was all. She totted a single grocery bag whose contents, now scattered about her, consisted of a half-pound package of penne, one half pint of cream cheese, a jar of pickled herring, and a half dozen fresh Kaiser rolls. She had almost reached the sidewalk, where she was to hang a left and walk the short way home. She lie with her emptied grocery bag pinned beneath her, between two straight lines meant for temporarily parking. That was the end of her, there, sprawled a quarter block from home, with a cranium awash with a sanguine tide that drowned every hope and dream she had ever known. I'm sure that after the ambulance left someone rescued the spilled groceries — the Kaiser rolls for sure, maybe even the herrings, if the jar hadn't broken. Evelyn was buried in Forest Lawn Hollywood Hills, just above the Warner Brothers Studios. She remains there to this day, the Warner Brothers too, the last time I pasted that way.

Never Forget

Nine-Eleven, the assassination of John F. Kennedy, Pearl Harbor, The Titanic, Sherman's burning of Atlanta, The Holocaust, the Khmer Rouge, Armenian genocide. Apartheid , Rwanda, The Crusades (from the Muslim point of view) the crucifixion of Jesus Christ, the Mongol hordes. On and on, century after century, the "Never Forget" list grows longer and longer. Cultures struggle under the weight of past injustices that "must not be forgotten". Who witnessing the tragedy of 9/11 directly or indirectly can ever forget it? The challenge is not to remember, but to forget, to throw off the irrational and proceed unburdened into the future in spite of the past. Give the past its due, then move on. The great tragedy of Nine-Eleven is our government's response to it, which, ironically, is what will be forgotten.

Over

Flipping the eggs in the frying pan she mutters: "It's over." He assumed she referred to his two over- easies. She was not. When he returned from work that evening she was not there, nor was she ever there again. Since then no eggs are eaten unless they are thoroughly beaten. It's never over-easy any more.

Panther in the Night

Met a black man in the dead of night
nearly undetectable to Caucasian's sight.
I knew he was there — his breathing,
sounded like — a panther seething. Though
blinded, I could plainly see, he was naked as
nakedness could be. From jungle primeval
with ebony sinew you're so fearful to see,
could I see you.

Shot dead

Daddy said the bad man with the beard was shot right through the head, dead. I guess it's always good when a bad man gets shot dead. But, it does make me kind of sad that anybody has to get shot dead in the head. Maybe the bad man had someone good, like a wife and kids, that really liked him and aren't glad he's dead; maybe even sad he's dead. It would be really sad if, no matter how bad he was, nobody cared that he was shot dead. My daddy and a bunch of this friends are going to throw a party to celebrate that hole in the bad man's head. He said I'd better stay in bed, 'cause there'd be lots of drinking, rough talk, and likely a few rounds shot in the air from his AK47, or maybe Uncle Fred's Uzi. He's my daddy and I love him but, sometimes he carries on just like my two year old brother Luger.

South of Calexico

There's this little town in Mexico, a few clicks
south of Calexico, wherein the third world
fades to a fourth. Villa-Lobos is seldom heard
here. Inhabitants are close to the earth
here, for nothing separates the citizen's
soles from the arid earth below them; and
pregnant fourteen year old girls lug splashing
water jugs a long way on dampened locks
too soon gray, while municipal corruption
partners with the Holy Roman Catholic
Church in a conspiracy to keep it just that
way. Wassily Kandinsky seldom comes up
in the daily conversation here. Feral dogs
gnaw meatless chicken bones expelled from
the portals of adobe huts by simple people
of simple means eating rice, scrawny fowl
and beans. Deprived equates with simplicity,
family and church the only path to felicity,
because there's simply nothing else. Or,
anything else in the vicinity 'cept the power
of the padre's erection, that functions
without a flow of electricity and nurtures
indigenous duplicty.

The Key

I am black and wear manacles on my sleeve. Hear them rattling, see them constraining me. The manacle key was lost at sea. So shackled, I sail on, held below, eating only heart and soul.

The Grin

Clara smiled to herself. He was dead and all she could do was smile to herself. Not the demonstrative type, she remained stoic throughout the ceremony. But there it was throughout, the smile only she could see. At the gravesite Clara was annoyed at the soft wet grass that would not support her spiked Gucci heals. Very sad indeed, she thought, this whole fucking charade, and too, the sin of my internal grin, not to mention ruining a $1300 pair of shoes. All in all though, it's safe to say, Clara now rests in peace.

The Lambs of God

(Josef Mengele's final hour.)

Prostrating himself before the One God, Josef cried out, "Lord of Hosts, forgive me for I have sinned." Seeing he was truly repentant, God forgave him. "Walk in the garden of the blessed, my son." As Josef took his last breath, he was at peace. High above, hearing the news, children playing in the fields of Elysium huddled together anxiously murmuring among themselves. "Fear not", assured the Good Shepherd, "for I and Josef will always be with you."

This rounds on me.

Two guys sitting in a bar with one empty
stool between them. Two rounds loosen
them up.
Jack says to Al: Hey man, what do you do?
Al: I'm a dragon slayer, how about you?
Jack: I'm a poet. Any work these days for a
dragon slayer?
Al: Not really. Haven't had a kill in a long
time. How about you, written any verses
lately? I mean sold any?
Jack: A few, but hardly anybody reads them
and nobody buys them. Haven't had a kill in
a long time.
Al: *How the hell do you make a living?*
Jack: I was just going to ask you the same
question.
Al: *I roll drunk poets in bars.*
Jack: What a coincidence, I roll drunk
dragon slayers anywhere I can find them.
Al: *No shit?*
Jack: No shit.
Al: *Hey old buddy, let me buy you another
drink.*
Jack: No way old buddy, this rounds on me.

Tootsie Pop

Some kid dropped a Tootsie Pop on the sidewalk. Musta been a girl 'cause a guy would have just picked it up and popped it back in his mouth just like nothin' happened which it didn't. Anyway, now there's a million ants on it, around it, running to and from it. I could plainly see the little fellas were just about as excited as ants can be at their good fortune that happened to be someone else's misfortune. I squatted down and watched the organized bedlam for about a half hour. Kinda reminded me of the riots in L.A. Finally getting bored, I had this great idea on how to liven things up. I poured lighter fluid on the sucker and the suckers and torched the lot. What a way to end a party, and they thought this was their lucky day. Kinda reminded me of the riots in L.A.

Who wrote these lines?

As a tear falls a year falls, and many more
of each will follow to call you up to lie down
and accept your sorrow: You gave far less
than you were given. And in the ground
newly riven, the sun shines despite you, the
moon shines without you. So it goes in the
Land of Oz, retake after retake — for God's
sake we'll never get it right. And that night I
drank myself to near oblivion. In the morning
— My lines! Oh God my lines. The lights are
hot. Who wrote this shit? Why am I wasting
my time learning these lines. Cut! Wait! Cut it
all! Back to the door on saw horses I use for a
writing table. Start anew, again. Who talked
me into this artless play? I remember when
there was excitement around every corner,
under every leaf, under every rock. Now, all
there is ... is — I can't remember my line. So
it's drivel, so fucking what. I used to be able
to remember drivel.
Let's see: Act 1, Scene 1, might as well
start here. Rewrite, dear Athena, save me
from myself. No leftovers in the frig. Fuck
it, I'll starve. Let's see, where was I ... Act1,
Scene1, line 1:
[Adam strolls on stage eating a burrito.]
Adam: "Damn, this is a one hell-of-a taco!"
Cut! Cut!

CREAM OF BROCCOLI SOUP

Cream of Broccoli Soup

So here's where all the trouble starts: In the
beginning, after just six days, there's still all
this unfinished business. God quit too soon.
I guess he didn't like getting his hands dirty.
So we have situations like when it's too cold
in the morning and too hot in the afternoon.
Who's fucking with the thermostat? Him
again. God, damn it, stop jiggling the knobs!
Find something else to do. In response, it
snowed all night. I bundle to the max for
my assault on the pristine drifts. I will be the
first to leave footprints on Mars. Great fun,
thank you God. This may seem unrelated,
but it isn't. You know, right and wrong stuff.
My grandfather admonished me: *Too much
whacking will drive you crazy.* I wanted to
respond that too little whacking is what
drives one crazy, but didn't. I'm sure he
knew. Those were the good old days, when
one thin dime could get you a shoe shine,
or a small glass of wine for the long walk
home. On that long walk home I once
encountered a duck that went quack!, I
expected that. Then that same duck said
the word QUACK! That I didn't expect.
A talking duck and in English too. But I
managed to reign in my excitement for one
word does not a talking duck make, any
more than one quack makes a man a duck.
I read that somewhere. When I finally arrived
home my mother asked, Do your homework
Billy? Why of course I did dear Mom, how

silly of you to ask. It's not so silly Billy, once upon a time you were my son. Where the hell did that come from? Menopause likely. Let me throw in this cryptic bit while there's a lull in the conversation. Did you know that the sun that shines also blinds. That not all broken hearts bleed. Or that not all flowers seed — no need, for not all laws bind. Did you also know, while we're on the subject of laws that: There's good and anti-good. When you take action, expect a reaction of equal intensity. We are forever bound by the laws of physics, until we discover a way of circumvention. Which brings me to this problem I have that is related to the laws of physics in that it involves motion, that is putting myself into motion. Moving forward, I continuously look back, finding myself tripping over the impediments that are right beneath my feet. I'm in a hurry to get over there. Over where exactly? Over there generally. My watch has no minute hand, it lurches ahead on the hour. A little scary. So here I am in a line that's way too long. Waiting is not my thing. So home I go empty handed, I'll return when the line is right. I return at a later date to find the doors closed. It is my fate that not even spiked locks and argyle socks will gain me entrance to those places to which I seek entry. But you know, shit happens. Take this buddy of mine. Joe tripped over a throw-rug and hit his head on the coffee table. Fucking coffee tables. Joe mellowed after that. Everyone

he meets he asks the same question: "Pick
a number between one and three, any
number". He doesn't deserve that. His wife's
the one who insisted on that wall-to-wall
glass top behemoth. Guess what, the bitch
divorced Joe on the grounds of diminished
capacity. He couldn't answer even the
simplest questions she claimed, like pick a
number between one and three. Some guys
never catch a break. Talk about catching a
break: Though Winter will not be denied and
fallen leaves populate the browned grass,
whatever's here will not last, eighty springs
have taught that. And with Spring comes
baseball. I've heard the Dodgers have a
rookie pitcher with a fastball that travels
near the speed of light, and hapless batters
have taken to swinging before the ball
leaves his hand. On the flip side, there's the
rookie playing in his first and ultimately
last Major League game who tried to steal
first base. I believe that's a record. And
then too, how last season ended: With two
outs and the winning run at third base, the
batted ball went straight up and came
straight down into the catcher's glove. The
man on third remained there for the rest of
his life. True story. Life can be so cruel. There
I go wandering all over the place. Please,
indulge me just a while longer. Now, the sky
is a bleached blue as is the surface of the
pool in which I wallow like a hapless hippo.
What the fuck's the problem? Reminds me
that deep sky blue was always my favorite

color. The very opposite of the darkness beneath my covers when it thunders. It was a day like any other, and the pond's mist rose up and decorated my argyle sweater with petals of dew. When the sun came out and the vapors vaporized, a voice called out to me: Please come join me down below. I have survived many days of wine and thorns, my borrowed time is now spent. On this very last day, I am deeply indebted to the almighty lender. Below, and when I say below I mean below, I lie in relative peace, except for the guy in the crypt next to me. He keeps rolling over and over in his coffin. Bare bones even on rayon make an awful racket. Stop! I shout, you're supposed to be dead. He doesn't respond. Really didn't expect him to being he has no vocal cords and all. My hope is when he turns to dust the sound will be greatly muffled, like sand passing through an hour glass. That's all for now. Maybe we can get together another time. Let me leave you with these few words: They told me God is the answer, I tried that, and it didn't work for me. I tried to wrap my head around the idea of death's nothingness. My head wouldn't stretch that far. Well I suppose it's like nothing you can know directly. I like to use the empty soap-can analogy. You open this can, pour out the contents, heat it up, then consume it. What's left? An empty soup can. There's a label on the can describing what the contents were, but now there's nothing in the can. That nothing in the can — that's you. By the way, if you don't mind me asking, what kind of soup were you? Cream of Broccoli. Really. Yes, I can see that. You certainly weren't chicken noodle.

***

Back There

A brisk winter breeze enters one ear swirls about counterclockwise (clockwise if I'm in the Southern Hemisphere) and exits the other ear. This refreshes the air in that vast cranial void, much like opening the windows in a summer cottage for the first time in nine months. On the quantum level this space teems with all manner of electromagnetic stuff, which seems to be of little use in my attempt to remember what day it is. Oh sure, I understand this is the area wherein ideas accrete, though I have no idea how this process works or even if it is still working. I do have a very clear idea that all's not right up there when I can't remember the dates of any of my four marriages, and the names of only two of my brides. But how useful is that information anyway? What I do remember, and what is so valuable to me now, is every detail of my childhood: names, places, events. I love going back there again. More and more often I pack up my things and make that trip. Of course, none of the clothes I pack here fit there. So what. You know, on one of these trips I'm just not coming back. I'm going to stay there. Sure I'll have to buy some new clothes, but so what. I can't wait to hear the sound of my corduroy knickers.

By Bonds

Chris sat on a park bench in a rain that fell mostly on his copious mane. Singular in his wetness, Chris was the only one visible in the park at 5am. Why would there be in weather like this. All-wet-Mark is in distress. What he had prepared for all his life, what was supposed to happen hadn't happened. Chris had prepared for everything but failure. Failure was never an option. From birth till a month ago the plan for success had succeeded. Then the fates took notice of this scenario so perfectly executed. Sensing hubris they became annoyed. What the fuck, thought they, this guy's got no respect, he's had it too easy. His boat's about to rock! Let's see if he can find his port in a typhoon. So it was that the rain began to fall, and fall and the sea became as tumultuous as in Noah's time. Chris became as a little child and cried for his mother and puked his guts out. Alas, those turned out to be the only guts he had. When the trial had ended, Chris was cost up on a park bench at 5am in the morning, where we find him now. Chris, have you any advice for us on how to weather a disaster like the one that has befallen you? "Yes I have", said Chris with a moist smirk, "Two words — By bonds!" Clearly, our drenched protagonist has not yet been defeated.

Father-Son Dialogue

A dying tiger moaned for a drink.
The tiger never dies, the moaning ever
abides. is a bird nest tersely undertaken
Beneath the covers the longing hovers.
It's a half-day boat we took —
Half of you and half of me put out to sea.
A gunny sack and a fresh squeeze of lemon,
the gaff *A sack for memories, juice to*
sweeten, and a hook to kill what soon would
be eaten — the last time we talked.
We talk now, as we did that day,
all about the one that got away.

Humming

I'm a voyeur and I've seen it all, all of it.
Some real disgusting shit going on out
there. But still, I cannot turn away. What am
I looking for? Chasing the first high? There
are no more highs, it's all subterranean now.
What I see everyone sees, and everyone
sees me. We all live in two places at once: in
our closet and on a hard drive tucked away
on the third floor of a building that has no
name and lots of subterranean conduit. On
a still dark night, if you're absolutely quiet,
you can hear a background hum. That
hum has nothing to do with the Big Bang
afterglow, that hum is you.

Isolation

Plato seldom ventures out after supper
(Dinner if you prefer). So safely ensconced is
Plato in what he knows. With his e-devices,
everything in the out-there is delivered to
him right in the cozy in-here without any risks
except maybe a power failure. To mitigate
the harshness of dramatized reality Plato
uses rugs to soften the hardwood floors,
draped windows with sheers to filter the light,
overstuffed furniture to soften the edges
and a HDTV 60" flat screen with its sharp
corners filed down, to let life in. Plato sits
there consumed by electromagnetic reality.
Plato loves being penetrated this way. So
there you have it, simply put, Plato's milieu,
in which he can see and experience you
without ever really knowing you. Hell, think
about it, almost all the people we know the
most about are dead: Mozart, Lincoln, Hitler.
Now if you'll excuse him, our man must take
a break. He'll lie his head down and marvel
at his good fortune at being free in his
crowded isolation. And just in case he were
to miss something, there's the DVR to call
back every pixel of his past life's streaming.

Josh

Josh is just your typical middle class, forty
something, modest y educated, directionless
fuck-up. Too harsh an analysis? Maybe,
but that's who he is. That's why he relies on
chemicals to propel him through the long
days. Josh is a Junior High School principal.
Just imagine, this dude in charge of our
youth's secondary education. Not only
that, Josh is mental pedophile. He has brain
fucked more fourteen year olds than almost
any man alive. Given his contorted mental
state, it is a wonder that Josh has never
once transgressed. How this is possible is
anyone's guess. Given these circumstances,
Josh's abstinence from evil should qualifies
him as a Saint, particularly being he's a
Roman Catholic. A statue of him should be
erected with him wearing a blindfold and an
unrequited erection. Future generations of
folks having heard of his trials would murmur
"Gosh Josh, how dic you not do it?" That's
in the future, for now the question is: Will
his abstinence continue? Can any man so
endure? God only knows, or should know
being he's the one who's contemplating
Canonization. Of course, to be canonized
on must first be dead. It all worked out
though. Josh mistakenly took some pills that
caused him to have an erection lasting
more than four hours, eight hours actually.
He passed from inadequate blood flow to
all but one of his extremities. Even in death

Josh remained an upright guy, which made it difficult to close the coffin lid. In the end, they had to lie St. Josh to rest lying on his side. On his left side I believe, being he was right handed. This is a true story.

***

Looking Good For God

Each Sunday morning I garnish my lithe form
with all manner of pomp and circumstance
in preparation for the parade before Jesus,
and more importantly, his followers. I thank
the Lord for this opportunity to pose and
pray, for all the eyes turned my way, and
for this splendid venue wherein the light
is always just right. I ask forgiveness on
behalf of those poor heathens dressed as
if to work in their gardens, who are always
squirmin' during the sermon, and prefer
the recessional to the processional. Thank
you too Lord, for all those beautiful young
lips that soundlessly articulate the hymn
on page one hundred and thirty-six, and
breathlessly gaze down at their newly
acquired two hundred dollar spiked heels.
Set them free Jesus, and allow me to lead
them on the path away from carnality
and bestiality. I know the way — I have
GPS. And before I forget, let me thank
you for my righteous cashmere sport coat
and saddle oxfords that set me so apart.
"What are saddle oxfords?" you ask, Dear
omniscient and omnipotent Father, with all
due respect, where have you been?

Marge

Marge the mouse looked into her full length dressing mirror and thought, I am fastidious about my personal appearance, hygiene, eat right, watch my weight. Hell, I'm downright cute, there's no getting around it, and I have a personality to match. Marge is generally a happy well-adjusted cute as the dickens little mouse. There is one thing though, that she just cannot abide, that is being called a rat. People can be so cruel. I have one question for those who in a panic use that expletive. Is Mickey Mouse a rat? Would you scream that word if it was Mickey who peeked from behind your refrigerator? I rest my case. So, in the future, if we should happen to meet, call me Marge, or Little Mouse, but never ever call me that word.

Tea

The Tea Party had a tea party and the guest list was a who's who of closed minds. The love of God and intolerance abounded there. Everyone danced and laughed at the finely nuanced off colored jokes and clever double entendres that flew between the revelers with the skill of code breakers. The next morning, cold tea-bags hung over half filled cups and the stale air was heavy with the sweet scent of sanctimony. Every attendee agreed, the party was a success. Like opinions were reaffirmed and inculcated, not the least of which were: Anglo Saxon sovereignty, manifest destiny, and Laissez-faire economics. A Nordic Jesus impersonator came by with long blond hair, wearing a scarlet cape with letters JC emblazoned there on, and did a standup routine that was outrageous. I'll bet you didn't know Jesus's father Joseph had a problem with erectile dysfunction? This could explain a lot of things. Anyway, thought you'd like to know about this affair. You all have a great evening now, and remember the Alamo, Pearl Harbor and … well, you know, all the rest of it. And may God (of the New Testament) bless America.

The Bell

Isabelle heard the bell, I know it, but she did not respond. She remained stiff and expressionless as if that two second ring had rung the light right out of her eyes. Finally the guys in the white coats came and hauled her manikin-like form away among murmurs and whispers and a giggle here and there. That bell had cast a spell on Isabelle for sure. "I think she's a witch", someone said. "Cool, maybe there's going to be an exorcism", said another. So it went on that day the bell took Isabelle away. I never saw her again, but I sure as hell will never forget her frozen there at 2:40pm on a Friday afternoon. Months later, a rumor surfaced that Isabelle had been raped by four boys that morning in a dark corner of the gym. That's all I know, and all I want to know about the day they took our sweet Isabelle away.

Toast

The toast was cold, the butter wasn't butter, the eggs ran, the coffee looked like tea, and the waitress was fat and sassy. What a way to start a day. With crumbs on my lap and grape jelly on my tie I hit the street. The food and service is ousy, but, it is convenient and cheap. I hate the place, but have breakfast there five times a week. There's great comfort in being served exactly what one expects on a regular basis. Like the abused wife, it's the continuity that keeps one coming back for more.

reflective pair

Two Joes

Joe lives in a battered old travel trailer
parked by tracks that are rusted from
neglect. Trains don't come this way
anymore. Joe lives with his insignificant
other Little Joe. They love each other,
at least that's what they tell each other.
Sometimes it's true, very often it isn't. Their
living conditions are by any standard
deplorable, but they take comfort in
knowing all the shit is theirs and that each
piece is time-stamped. They live mostly in
the past. Looking at their present, is it any
wonder they prefer another time? The Joes
want one thing more than any other — to
be left alone. This is usually no problem,
their domain presents a formidable barrier
of sight and smell. They've had pets in the
past, but they just seem to disappear. There
have been doubts. Both Joe and Little Joe
have had encounters with the heterosexual
establishment. Both had wives who were
mortified when their mates changed sides.
Neither wife has gotten over it. Both men are
not totally over it either. Each has wondered,
separately, if maybe it would have been
better to suppress the sexual thing, live a lie
and have clean socks to wear and a place
to stay that the pigs hadn't abandoned
because of the unsanitary living conditions.
Hey! Fuck you for second guessing our life-
choices. Fuck you for taking a shower every
day. Fuck you for trimming your toenails.
Fuck you for having indoor plumbing.

We, Little Joe and me, are knee deep in
freedom. We answer to no one, we scratch
our ball and pick or noses with impunity. We
piss where ever and whenever we chose.
Is this a great country or what? God bless
America and watch out for the abandoned
well and our housekeeper who went missing
three months ago.

***

Never in the history of man has there been total peace. He is programed to live in homogenous groups of extended families, suspicious of all those who don't qualify, and more than willing to kill anyone who tramples his sod. Things haven't changed much. Even in so-called civilized societies there is violence all around. Murder is broken down into two categories: There is murder without mayhem – this is acceptable, like if you murder your wife. Then you have your murder with mayhem – a far more despicable act. An example of this would be the events of 9-11. When you have been mayhemed, you have the right, or let's say the duty to mayhem in return with even greater instensity. This revenge thing is not likely to end anytime soon. How do these comments qualify as an epilogue to this book? Hey dude, that's my decision. I call your question uncalled for. You're not from around here are you?

The last last word: AMEN

Other books by this author:

Dead Serious
99 Cents Worth
From My Stoop
Beach Boulevard
Zig Zag #1 and the Holy Rolling
Catholic Church
The Reflective Pair
Act 5
Her, Him, Them, and the Others
Cream of Broccoli Soup

Some of these books can be orderd through
B&N.com or Amazon.com

www.ingramcontent.com/pod-product-compliance
Lightning Source LLC
Chambersburg PA
CBHW032036080426
42733CB00006B/103